The

Peninsula State Park

History and Stories

By: Norman R. Aulabaugh

Valley View Publishing
Orfordville, Wisconsin

The Park

By: Norman R. Aulabaugh

First Edition

Published by:

Valley View Publishing
2541 S Tollefson Road
Orfordville, WI 53576-9443

608 879-2841

vvpublishing@ticon.net
(vee vee publishing)

ISBN: 0-9785293-0-8

Cover watercolor by Kathy Glasnap.

Kathy Glasnap, professional watercolorist for 36 years, works out of her gallery in the woods located on County Highway A, three-quarters of a mile south of the intersection with County Road F outside Fish Creek, Wisconsin. Kathy Glasnap has had her works featured on the cover of the Key to the Door and has done work for the National Wildlife Federation. Kathy blends the intricate detail of architectural designs with the gentle nature of the landscape to capture the beauty of Door County.

Printed by:

Terry Printing, Janesville, Wisconsin

Dedication

I dedicate this book to my father who "discovered" this park and began our family tradition of vacationing in The Park every summer. I also dedicate this book to my mother Vivian and sister Sandy who never objected to having The Park be the only family vacation choice to be considered each year. And finally, I dedicate this book to my present camping family; my wife Carol and our dog Sandy (no relation to my sister) that are my camping partners today.

Acknowledgements

I thank my wife, Carol, for the many ways she helped in organizing the material for this book. And I want to thank my mpc computer and Microsoft Word, without which I could never have completed this project. Even though my computer helped me immensely, it was also the source of much frustration when margins, page numbers and countless other things "went south" and caused me to seek advice from Phyllis Anderson to help me get things back on track again.

Special thanks go to Kathleen Harris, naturalist at Peninsula State Park who gave me access to The Park memories book, found park photos when I needed them, and made suggestions for changes in parts of the text. Thanks to Gary Soule and Carl Johnson for supplying photos. I thank Kathy Glasnap for the cover art work. But most of all, I thank The Park and the people we camped with over the years for providing the stories I have recorded in this book I simply call "The Park."

Table of Contents

Table of contents continued

The Preface

The title of this book is "The Park" with the emphasis being on **"THE."** When I say "The Park," I mean Peninsula State Park, not Yellowstone, not Yosemite, or any other park. When anyone in my family said "The Park" we all knew this meant Peninsula State Park. Throughout this book, I will always refer to Peninsula State Park as The Park!

In 1974, I decided I was going to write a book about The Park – someday. In 1991, I began by collecting interviews on tape and wrote a few chapters. Each year, I discovered more material about The Park. A few years ago, I almost gave up on the idea of this book. Everything that could be said about The Park had been said. But one day, I talked to a lady at the Door County Historical Museum in Sturgeon Bay who encouraged me to continue by saying, "You will probably take a different approach than other writers." That comment gave me the will to continue. Doing the research has been fun. There have been countless visits to Door County Libraries, to the University of Wisconsin Memorial Library at Madison, Wisconsin and to the State Historical Society Library. Some of the people I interviewed as many as fifteen years ago are no longer living. My pile of research material including three notebooks, a stack of audio tapes and old photos, is now one of my prized possessions.

I wrote this book because I had to satisfy a need to express my feelings for This Park. Now that the writing is complete, that need is satisfied. But my desire to actually be in The Park is not satisfied. As soon as I turn this text over to the printer, Carol and I are leaving for two weeks of camping in The Park.

All profit I may receive from the sale of this book will be donated to Peninsula State Park. Carol and I can think of no better way to express our appreciation for this enchanted place we still simply call, The Park.

VIII

One

The Introduction

"Old winds are about tonight, old steps up the street. It's not long a human lives, but the place underneath stays, through all those changes made." Warren Nelson wrote this line in a song called "Old Winds." Whenever I walk the path between the Nicolet Bay boat ramp and the beach, I remember this line from "Old Winds."

If I could be anywhere in The Park, where would I be? On top of Eagle Tower? On Sven's Bluff at sunset? Somewhere on Eagle Trail? In camp at site 636? It's a tough decision, but my first choice would be that small section of path along Nicolet Bay. "The place underneath stays, through all those changes made."

How many people have walked and bicycled this path? It does not matter. The place underneath stays. The cedar trees never change. The view of the beach, Horseshoe Island and Eagle Bluff is always the same. I walked this path with my mother, father and sister over fifty years ago on our way to a Saturday evening campfire program of songs and stories. Tents were pitched back in the trees. There are still tents among those same trees today. Years later, when the Nicolet Bay Store opened, my father and I walked this path to buy a Drumstick after dinner. Drumsticks are now called Sundae Cones, but the path has never changed. "It's not long a human lives." My mother and father are gone. But the path remains the same. I walked this path with my new bride Carol, when we honeymooned in the Park in 1970. Carol and I walk the same path today. We have changed, but the path has remained the same. If I could be anywhere in The Park, it would be on this path.

Whenever I return to The Park, intense feelings of nostalgia overwhelm me. The feeling starts when I start to descend the hill leading into Fish Creek. If the radio is playing, I turn it off. Conversation stops. As I turn into The Park from Highway 42, my heartbeat quickens. After checking in at the office, I drive down Shore Road lined with the same ancient cedar trees I saw on my first trip to The Park in

1950. I roll the window down and breathe in the scent of the trees, the earth and the bay. I'm back. I have returned to a place that stays, "through all those changes made."

If my time was short and I was recalling things I should have done but didn't, this book would be at the top of my list. I have felt the need to pull together this story of The Park for years. I have now satisfied that need. But my feelings for The Park have not changed. If I could be anywhere right now, I would be on that path along Nicolet Bay. This is a story of Peninsula State Park. "Through all those changes made, the place underneath stays."

Two

THE GEOLOGY

Door County begins just north of Algoma. But to me and my wife Carol, Door County really begins when we descend the hill leading into Fish Creek on Highway 42. At this point you descend a bluff and truly start to get a feel for the geology of the area. The road is cut into the limestone that forms the backbone of the peninsula. You get a quick glimpse of the outline of the harbor at Fish Creek and begin to see how the bluffs, points, bays, and open water merge to form that perpetual and never-ending picture of Door County.

Shapes make connections in our minds. The gentle curve of a shoreline, leading outward toward a point of land and a white pebble beach separating the blue waters from a high limestone bluff, is an image that belongs to Door County. The polished white rocks of the shoreline can be identified in an instant by anyone who has been on that shoreline. A few of these rocks have traveled home with us and are mixed with rocks gathered from other places we have visited. I can spot the Door County rocks from among the others in an instant.

A Robert Leland Pence print titled "Tennison Bay - Peninsula Park" hangs in our living room. The inscription on the back states, "Shortly after you enter the park from the Fish Creek entrance, the road nearly borders the water's edge. It is a very picturesque spot and almost always invites a layover. You may look for that special stone, or just sit, gaze at the water, and listen to the gulls." The white band of small rocks that separate the water from the land is clearly visible in this print as is the gentle curve of the land forming Tennison Bay.

We have a Jack Anderson watercolor titled "Bayside Snowfall." Again, a narrow strip of white rock separates the blue water from the land. Trees outline the bluff that projects into the water. It is unmistakably Door County. We have a seriograph done by B. Cook titled "Sunset Sail" and many watercolors done by Kathy Glasnap. In all of these, there is that same shoreline, so distinctive to Door County. It's the geology of Door County that makes it unique.

The limestone spine of the peninsula is magnificently exposed at Eagle Bluff. Eagle Bluff is splendid at sunrise when viewed from the Ephraim side, and more magnificent at sunset, when viewed from the north shore of Nicolet Bay. As the sun sets, the trees on the bluff first turn brilliantly green, next the limestone radiates pure white, and finally it reflects all the colors of the fading sunset.

I often thought there was no other place in the world like Eagle Bluff in Peninsula State Park. Then one summer, while taking a driving vacation circling Lake Superior, we happened to stop at Fayette, in Michigan's Upper Peninsula, separated from Door County by Lake Michigan water dotted with island stepping stones; Washington, Rock, St. Martin, Poverty and Summer Islands. While standing on the shore at Fayette, the site of a century-old iron smelting town, I found myself gazing at a mirror image of Eagle Bluff. Surely this image was a mirage. But it wasn't. It was simply that same limestone skeleton, emerging from the water at that point, forming another peninsula, this one reaching out, trying to join with its counterpart, fifty miles to the south in Door County. I needed to learn more about the geology of The Park.

The oldest rocks on earth date back to the Cambrian periods of geologic time and are over 520 million years old. Rocks of this age are exposed at different places on earth. One large exposure is the Canadian Shield which covers much of Canada. This "Shield" extends down through the Upper Peninsula of Michigan and into the northern parts of Wisconsin. But at The Park, these ancient rocks are 1850 feet below the surface covered with layers of limestone, sandstone and shale. Long ago, warm shallow seas eroded these Cambrian rocks. This erosion process created sedimentary deposits which formed sandstone and shale in the Ordovician period over 438 million years ago. Later, in the Silurian period, which lasted for the next 30 million years, water levels around the world rose when a period of glaciation at the South Pole ended. The earliest known land plants and insects date back to this age. Egad, the first mosquitoes in The Park! A very hard form of limestone known as dolomite was formed in the Silurian Seas on top of the sandstone and shale formed in the Ordovician period. This limestone is 600 feet thick in Door County.

Even though the limestone of Door County is hard and resistant to erosion, water, over time, will make its mark. Ancient rivers flowed over the area prior to the emergence of glaciers in Wisconsin. Remember, the features that we see today such as Green Bay and Lake Michigan were not yet formed. It is generally believed there was a river flowing south through what is now the middle of Lake Michigan. Other rivers flowed into this ancient Michigan River from the west, some of them cutting across what is now the Door County Peninsula. If you look at a map, you can easily see how the ancient Menominee River flowing in a south-eastward direction across the area which is now Green Bay and through the area which is now Sturgeon Bay made a cut in the peninsula. Other cuts made by other ancient rivers are evident between Ellison Bay and Rowley Bay, Sister Bay and North Bay, and Eagle Harbor and Baileys Harbor. It is no small coincidence that the bays on the peninsula usually occur in pairs; the one on the Green Bay side being just a little north of the corresponding bay on the Lake Michigan side.

Next a lifting of the land occurred. Such a tilting or gentle uplifting of the land is called a cuesta, and erosion of the edge of this cuesta formed the geologic feature we call the Niagara Escarpment. An escarpment is simply the steep eroded face of a cuesta. The Niagara Escarpment extends all the way from Wisconsin, across Michigan, into Canada, and dips back into the United States in New York where it forms the rock base for Niagara Falls. An early visitor to Door County, Increase A. Lapham, was one of the first people to recognize that this escarpment was one continuous feature extending this entire distance.

If the underlying rock of an escarpment is soft, as is the soft sandstone and shale underlying the limestone in Door County, this soft rock will erode and wear away causing the hard limestone to tumble down forming a cliff. This is the process which made the steep rock cliffs that we see in Peninsula State Park today.

As the escarpment crumbled away it retreated eastward. A few outliers or "islands" were formed when the rock underneath did not erode causing the upper layers to collapse. Chambers Island is an example of such an outlier that provides a beautiful backdrop for watching sunsets from Sven's Bluff.

The Niagara Escarpment was well-formed when the Ice Age and successive periods of glaciers began a little over a million years ago. Different stages of ice advances occurred as the climate warmed and then cooled again and again. The earliest ice advance was the Nebraskan stage followed by the Kansan, the Illinoian and finally the Wisconsin. With the Wisconsin Glacier, there were two lobes of the glacial ice sheet that covered the northeast portion of Wisconsin. The Green Bay lobe scraped out and formed the basin we now know as Green Bay. The Lake Michigan lobe did likewise a little further east. The Door Peninsula split the ice advance into the two lobes mentioned. The ice abraded the escarpment, but the hard dolomite withstood the advance. The fissure formed between these two advancing lobes, split because of the Door Peninsula, created some magnificent landforms south of Door County that can be seen in the Kettle Moraine.

Evidence of glacier activity can be found in The Park. Glacial erratics are rocks that are not normally found in an area, but were carried to the area by the glaciers and then left there as the ice melted and retreated. There is an excellent example of such an erratic right next to the front door of the nature center in The Park with an interesting story recorded on an accompanying sign on how the rock came to that particular location.

As the glaciers advanced and retreated, the normal outlets for water to flow from the area were often blocked. Times of very high water levels occurred when glaciers blocked the flow of water to the east through the outlet now known as the St. Lawrence River. The water levels rose until it flowed out the south end of Lake Michigan, down the Des Plaines River, and finally into the Mississippi River. It took until the early nineteen hundreds for the same feat to be repeated, this time with the help of the Army Corps of Engineers to reverse the flow of water on the Chicago River!

Photo, Gary Soule and the Door County Maritime Museum.

With high lake levels caused by normal outlets being blocked with ice, features such as the sea cave, commonly called Eagle Cave, were created by wave action and now stand high and dry well above today's water level. Besides the cave high up on Eagle Bluff, you can find sea caves being created today at Cave Point County Park just south of Jacksonport on the Lake Michigan side of the peninsula.

The 1919 picture above shows early park visitors at Eagle Cave. The steps are no longer there.

Gary Soule describes the interior of the cave as being 41 feet in depth. Gary is a member of the American Spelean History Association and was the curator of the Door County Maritime Museum in Sturgeon Bay when it was located at the foot of Florida Street next to Sunset Park.

As the ice melted, removing its enormous weight from the land, glacial rebound, or a rising of the land, occurred. Such rebound, over time, has produced many different lake levels and resultant different shorelines that can still be located in The Park if you take the time to look and use your imagination. A trip to the Ridges Sanctuary at Baileys Harbor is highly recommended. The Ridges Sanctuary contains over 29 swales that give evidence to changing water levels in more recent times.

The ice age ended in Wisconsin about twelve thousand years ago. This was about the same time the first people came to America crossing over from Siberia to Alaska on a land bridge exposed because of a period of low water levels. These people are referred to as the Paleo Indians and were probably the first human visitors to Wisconsin and surely the first campers in The Park!

Three

The Native Americans

The first visitors to The Park were Native Americans. Even though we have no written record of their history and travels, surely they passed through the woods, along the shores of and even camped in what is now Peninsula State Park. The moccasin trails of these Native Americans were the first trails in The Park. Many different Native American cultures lived in the area of the Great Lakes. Some of the cultures and their time periods are:

Paleo	13,000 BC	to	4,000	BC
Copper	3,000 BC	to	500	BC
Woodland	1,000 BC	to	1634	AD
Mississippi	800 BC	to	1600	AD
Historic	1634 AD	to	PRESENT	

The Paleo culture, descendants of the first emigrants to North America who crossed the Bering Straight land bridge, ventured into what is now

Wisconsin following the end of the last glacier ice advance some fifteen thousand years ago. The early Paleo culture is found at only one site in Door County south of the ship canal in Sturgeon Bay. Evidence of early Woodland culture sites have been found at North Bay, at the top of the Peninsula at Porte de Morts, and on Washington Island. Late Woodland cultures have been found at Heinz Creek and at Whitefish Dunes State Park.

Three archaeological sites identified by the State of Wisconsin Historical Society are found in the vicinity of Nicolet Bay. The Park was excavating for new vault toilets near the beach in 1990. Victoria Dirst, an archaeologist with the State of Wisconsin, surveyed the site and found remnants to indicate the presence of Woodland and Oneota campsites and perhaps even a prehistoric village at this site. Dirst found chert flakes and points, undecorated woodland and Oneota shards and bone fragments. The Oneota were the prehistoric ancestors of several modern Native American groups of the Mississippi culture time period that established villages around Green Bay, Lake Winnebago, Lake Koshkonong, and La Crosse.

Much of what probably remains from early Indian settlements in Door County has been lost. Native Americans liked to settle at places with good harbors and sand beaches which made it easy for them to launch their canoes. Unfortunately, the early European settlers also favored these same locations. Much of what we could have learned about the early people who lived in Door County probably lies beneath the streets of Sturgeon Bay, Sister Bay, Ephraim and other Door County villages. It's ironic, that the same thing occurred to some extent at Nicolet Bay. The sand and gravel removed from the excavation for the toilets in Nicolet Bay was probably used as fill for the driving range parking lot at the golf course. Like the artifacts that may lie under some streets of Door County villages, artifacts from the Nicolet Bay site may now lie under the asphalt at the golf course driving range.

The historic period dates from the year Jean Nicolet met the Winnebago, who called themselves Hochungra, or First People, on the shores of Green Bay at Red Banks. One of the archaeological sites in Nicolet Bay is a possible stopping place of Jean Nicolet in 1634. In his writings, Nicolet said he stopped for a week at a site which was two days travel north of Red Banks. It is about a two day trip from Nicolet Bay down to the Red Banks by canoe. I wonder if Nicolet had trouble making a reservation for his campsite!

Most of the activity in the historic period involved migrations of different tribes through the Door Peninsula. These migrations were movements of Native Americans in and out of different areas, particularly from the eastern United States. The eastern tribes could now come freely into Wisconsin, because the numbers of the once powerful Winnebago in the area at the time Nicolet visited had declined, probably because of being infected with European diseases for which they had no biological defense. By 1668 there were few Winnebago left in Door County. Many had migrated south and were living in the Rock River Valley around Lake Koshkonong. The Potawatomi then became the main tribe in the area.

The early Algonquian lived in the area of the St. Lawrence River. The Algonquian were pushed westward by the Iroquois who had obtained guns through early trade with the settlers on the eastern seaboard. The Algonquians merged with other tribes and became known as the Ottawa.

The Ottawa settled on Washington Island with a few Huron in 1650. The Potawatomi were living on Washington Island in 1670 and were migrating southward. For many years, the Potawatomi had villages on Washington, Rock, and Detroit Islands. They were living on these islands when LaSalle visited this area in 1679.

The Salk had lived in the Door County area for awhile, having been forced from their land in Michigan by the Chippewa. The Salk warred with the Menominee and were eventually forced southward. The Chippewa also forced the Fox south where they eventually settled with the Salk.

Native Americans continued to live in the area of the city of Green Bay until the early 1900s, but by this time, the large settlements that had existed on Washington Island, Rock Island, and Detroit Island were gone. As the European settlers came to harvest lumber, fish and farm, the presence of Native Americans in the area declined.

A memorial pole honoring Door County's Native Americans was dedicated at The Park Golf Course in 1927. The unveiling was done by Potawatomi Chief Simon Kahquados.   At the unveiling, Chief Kahquados said, "We have never looked for any honor from the white people and we have not received any. We are therefore grateful that there are men who look with respect upon our fathers and have raised this pole as a visible sign."

Chief Kahquados (1851 to 1930) is buried close to the Memorial Pole. The inscription on his marker states – "This stone marks the grave of Simon Onanguisse Kahquados head Chief of the Potawatomi Indians. He was the last descendent of a line of Chiefs who ruled over the Door County Peninsula for many centuries. A true and worthy Indian."

What we need to know and respect today, is that these Native Americans were the keepers of the land long before Jean Nicolet first set foot upon the shore at Red Banks. The struggles, hardships, and confrontations that followed, make up the time period we now call historic. Only recently, have we come to realize and respect the wisdom and intellectual insight inherent in many of the great Native American leaders.

Many stories of the Native Americans and early explorers from the historic period can be found in the book, "Up Country, Voices from the Midwestern Wilderness," compiled and edited by William Joseph Seno, and published by Round River Publishing Company, Madison, Wisconsin. This book is a compilation of journals, letters, and memoirs of such people as Pierre Esprit Radisson, Father Claude Allouez, Father Jacques Marquette, Father Louis Hennepin, Henri De Tonty and Chief Black Hawk just to name a few. An excellent account of Wisconsin Indians including a history of their lands and treaty history has been compiled in Nancy Oestreich Lurie's book, "Wisconsin Indians," Published by the State Historical Society of Wisconsin.

Four

The History – B.P. (Before Park)

In 1900, 250 acres became Interstate Park, the first state park in Wisconsin. It would be ten more years before the next park, Peninsula State Park, would be created.

Wisconsin Governor Robert LaFollette appointed a commission in 1903 to look at the possibility of establishing a state park at Devil's Lake. The Devil's Lake area almost became Wisconsin's second state park if it had not been for the work of Tom Reynolds.

Thomas Reynolds, who emigrated from Ireland in 1866, is often called the father of Peninsula State Park. Reynolds, who farmed near Jacksonport in Door County, was elected to the State Assembly in 1906 when the legislature was considering a bill to create a state park at Devil's Lake. Tom Reynolds just happened to be with United States Senator Isaac Stephenson the day the entire state legislature was visiting Devil's Lake. Reynolds spoke to Senator Stephenson proclaiming that Door County had places that were much more suited to become a state park than Devil's Lake. Senator Stephenson was interested. Reynolds pushed the subject and asked Senator Stephenson if he would be willing to donate some money to help establish a state park in Door County. The Senator said he would. A few days later, Tom Reynolds introduced a bill in the Wisconsin legislature to appropriate $75,000 to be used to acquire land in Door County to establish a state park.

The legislature was skeptical. Door County was a remote place. Devil's Lake was close to Madison. But in politics, money talks! Because Reynolds had secured a promise from Senator Stephenson to donate money for a Door County park, he was able to tell the legislature that $25,000 would be given by the good Senator to help create the park. Reynolds' bill passed and $75,000 was authorized to purchase land for a new state park.

United States Senator Stephenson was expecting the new park to be named after him. After all, he had pledged $25,000 to help establish the park. But politics entered again. Robert LaFollette, the great progressive, had just moved on to the United States Senate after having served for six years as Governor of Wisconsin. Stephenson was a staunch conservative. There were many LaFollette supporters serving in Wisconsin's legislature. They were not very eager to name a new state park after the conservative Senator Stephenson. Senator Stephenson's money was returned, but the $75,000 appropriation remained. This appropriation may never have passed had it not been for Stephenson's generous offer to donate $25,000 to help acquire land. Regardless, the process to create a new state park had been initiated. This is why many claim that Tom Reynolds and to a somewhat lesser degree, Senator Stephenson, should be considered the fathers of Peninsula State Park.

Reynolds wanted three areas in Door County to be considered for a park. His first choice was an area at Clark Lake, his second an area at Kangaroo Lake and last on his list was the peninsula between Fish Creek and Ephraim. However, a state park board formed in 1907 would have the final say on this matter.

In 1907, chapter 495 of the laws passed by the legislature in Wisconsin called for the establishment of a state park board to make recommendations on acquiring land for establishing new parks. The board hired John Nolen to assist in their effort.

John Nolen (1869-1937), a renowned city planner and landscape architect from Cambridge, Massachusetts, was a man with great vision. People with great vision accomplish great things. Nolen took a garden approach to planning. He believed in recreational space. Nolan did planning for Janesville, Wisconsin, which now calls itself "The City of Parks." A major thoroughfare in Madison, Wisconsin, was named John Nolan Drive in honor of the fine work he did there. But no park in Janesville or Madison can top Nolan's work which helped establish three great Wisconsin Parks.

The state park board, consisting of T.E. Brittingham of Madison, E.E. Browne of Waupaca and W.H. McFetridge of Baraboo submitted

John Nolan's report on January 13, 1909. A portion of the introduction to their report says it all:

"The park board have attempted to sound the sentiment of the people of the state in regard to the establishment of state parks and find, among all classes of people, a strong, abiding sentiment in favor of the state establishing parks and thus preserving the great natural beauties with which this state has been endowed, from commercial vandalism or private ownership. We believe that the state should act while the property desired can be purchased at a reasonable figure and at a price which would prove an excellent investment from a purely money standpoint, and that if action is postponed, it will be more difficult each year to acquire these beauty spots that are already beginning to attract the attention of wealthy lovers of nature all over the world."

Nolan was wise to point out the main requirement for a state park which distinguished it from other entities such as a state forest. Nolan wrote that the purpose of a park, "is to refresh and strengthen and renew tired people, to fit them for the common round of daily life."

Not too many years ago, I was the manufacturing manager for a company in Janesville, Wisconsin, that made parts for the automobile industry. This was a pressure cooker job. When I thought I could stand it no more, a week of camping at Peninsula State Park would renew my spirit. A tent, a sleeping bag, a campfire and the serene setting of The Park renewed me. John Nolan truly identified the purpose of a park.

Today, a small parcel of land with a hundred feet of shoreline in Door County can sell for more than one million dollars. In 1909 John Nolan wrote, "I found leagues and leagues together of the shore line to be all private holdings, without the intervention, in these long reaches, of a rod of space on the shore to which the public has a right to go." Had it not been for Nolan's work, this could have been the case with all the shoreline in Peninsula State Park today.

John Nolan had a vision. Nolan surveyed four locations in Wisconsin: the dells of the Wisconsin River at Kilbourn, Devil's Lake near Baraboo, various properties in Door County endorsed by Thomas Reynolds and the bluffs where the Wisconsin River flows into the Mississippi just south of Prairie du Chien.

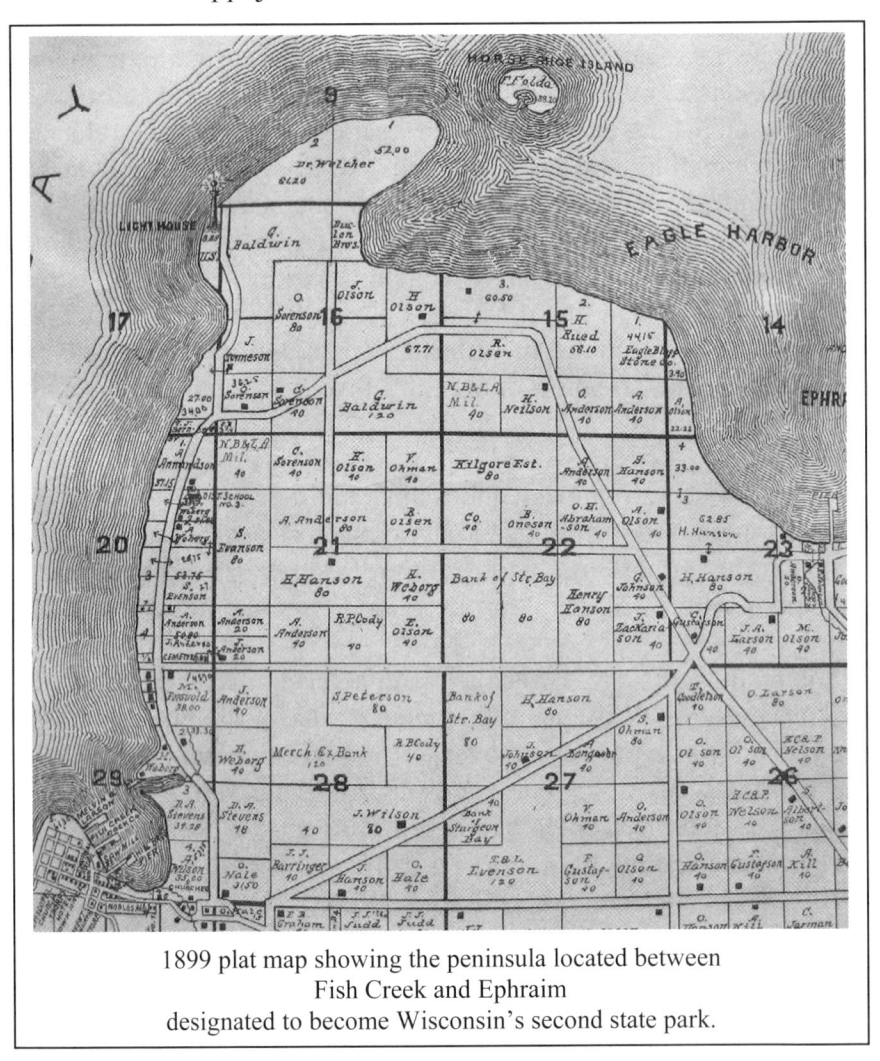

1899 plat map showing the peninsula located between
Fish Creek and Ephraim
designated to become Wisconsin's second state park.

In describing the possible sites in Door County, Nolan wrote, "But it is the opinion of the State Park Board that the finely situated peninsula between Ephraim and Fish Creek and north of the diagonal road, including some 3,800 acres, more than eight miles of shore line with a number of deep water harbors, will constitute an adequate and unified State Park. In this view I concur. Such a tract would cost, it is estimated, not more than $75,000, an average of less than $20 an acre (options have already been obtained for 2,200 acres for $35,000). Beyond all question the climate is healthful, invigorating and tonic, quickly bracing tired bodies and nerves."

You will find no better description of Peninsula State Park than that written by John Nolan in his report. "Reminding one constantly of the coast of Maine, the shore with its many graceful indentations is a never-ending delight. It sweeps from point to point, here a beach of fine sand, there of gravel, then, in contrast, precipitous limestone bluffs, rising to a height of a hundred feet or more covered with a heavy growth of native trees and shrubs, mostly evergreen. Almost at each step on the land, each boat's length on the water, a new vista is opened, a new composition is afforded. With a temperature always moderate, the purest of air laden with the fragrance of balsam and pine, with unexcelled facilities for sailing, boating, fishing . . . this Door County region under State control might become a famous pleasure resort of the highest order."

The commission supported their argument to acquire land for state parks with authoritative letters. John Woodbury, Secretary of the Commonwealth of Massachusetts Metropolitan Commission, urged the Wisconsin Legislature to acquire park land. He argued that delaying any decision would jeopardize the proposed parks because possible land would become built up and therefore become too expensive to obtain.

University of Wisconsin President, Charles R. Van Hiss, wrote a letter advocating acquiring land for parks that fit perfectly with John Nolan's view that the purpose of a park was to refresh and strengthen the spirit. Van Hiss argued that Wisconsin formerly had large uninhabited tracts of land people could use as camping grounds and where they could "go for relief from their cares." Hiss warned that these uninhabited areas would soon be private land. Therefore it was imperative the state acquire lands for public purposes.

Van Hiss's words, "Camping grounds have been places where men and women could go for relief from their cares;" are so true. My father, as he sat by his campfire, cooking chicken over cedar coals, would gaze out over Nicolet Bay toward Eagle Bluff and say, "I ain't mad at nobody."

Governor Robert LaFollette had moved on to the United States Senate. In July of 1909, the Wisconsin State Park Board passed a resolution asking Governor Davidson for approval to purchase land for what would soon be Peninsula State Park. The original appropriation was for $75,000. But another $21,000 went for improvements including a new road between Fish Creek and Ephraim. Peninsula became the second Wisconsin State Park.

The state park board did not select Tom Reynolds' first or second choice of a location for a park. But they did pick his third choice to become Peninsula State Park in 1910. Devil's Lake became the third state park in 1911. The bluffs and adjacent land, where the Wisconsin flows into the Mississippi, became Wyalusing State Park in 1917.

As for the dells, it was realized that the best time for action had passed. The dam under construction at Kilbourn, now called the Wisconsin Dells, had raised the water level covering many of the scenic formations on the Wisconsin River. Commercial activity in the area had driven up the price of land making it too expensive to acquire for park purposes. Nolan and the state park board were wise to urge action on land acquisition at the other areas where it was not already too late.

Thank you, Tom Reynolds, Senator Stephenson, John Nolan and the state park board for helping to make sure the land on the peninsula between Ephraim and Fish Creek became Wisconsin's second state park.

Five

The Land

The resolution to establish The Park had been passed in July of 1909. The process of acquiring options on land had already begun. An 1899 plat map of the area shows over 70 individually surveyed parcels of land in the area designated to become The Park. Many of these were undeveloped vacant land and a single individual often owned multiple parcels. Newspaper articles of the time indicate about 40 families and other owners were making a living from their holdings in the area designated for The Park.

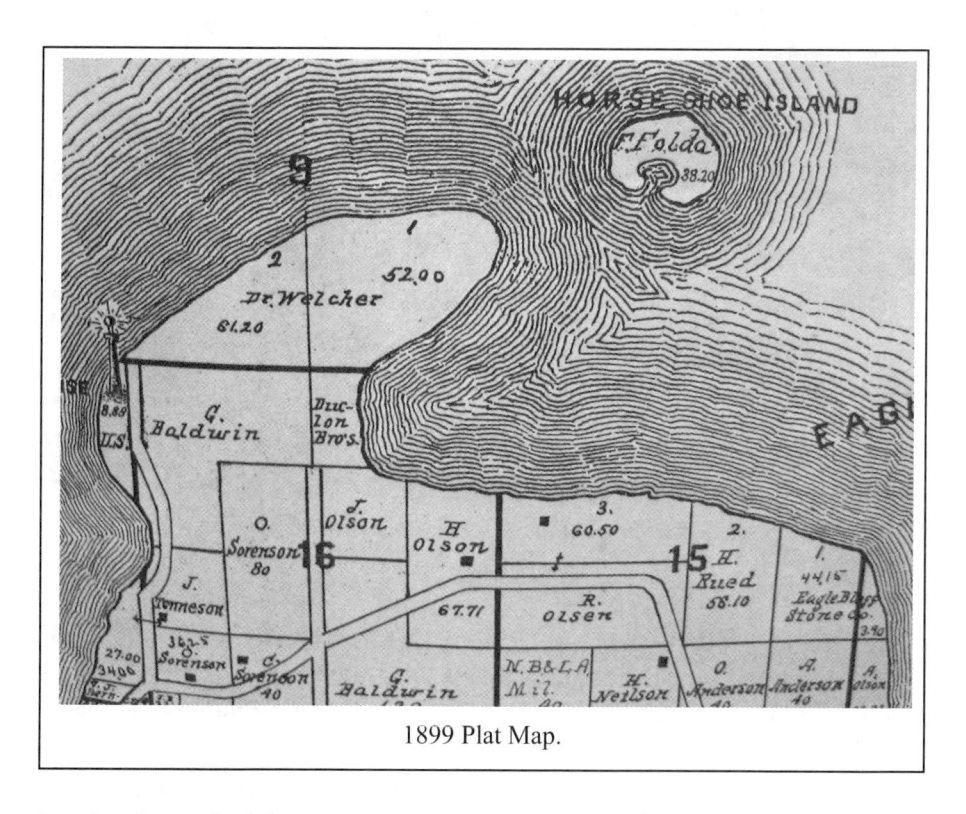

1899 Plat Map.

Dr. Herman Welcker owned 52 acres now called Welcker's Point. Dr. Welcker, a German immigrant, established himself in the tourist business in Fish Creek in 1898 and later moved a large building across Green Bay from Menominee, Michigan to be used as a hotel.

The building is now known as the Whistling Swan. Other accommodations for his guests included cottages which are now part of the White Gull Inn.

Ole B. Olson owned the land which included the beach at Nicolet Bay (J. Olson on the map). The Hans Olson farm was on 68 acres immediately east of the Ole B. Olson property which is now the 800 numbered campsites in Nicolet Bay and originally the farm of Ole Larson.

The Ole Larson Homestead at Nicolet Bay.
Photo, Peninsula State Park.

The Duclon brothers from the Eagle Bluff lighthouse owned land now in the vicinity of what is now the boat launch ramp at Nicolet Bay. The Eagle Bluff Stone Company owned 48 acres at Eagle Bluff where Eagle Terrace is now located. Hjalmar Holand owned 56 acres just west of the Stone Company property including the shore line in the area where the Minnehaha Trail intersects with Eagle Trail (H. Rued on the map). Tenneson owned the property at Tennison Bay (note again differences in spelling) where the campground is now located.

Sven Amundson owned the land now known as Sven's Bluff. District School # 3 had a schoolhouse on Shore Road just south of Sven's Bluff. Vida and Ella Weborg, living next door, were the schoolteach-ers. The Simon Even-son farm, which later would become the site of Camp Meenahga, was located along Shore Road south of the old school. Henry Weborg owned land at Weborg's Point.

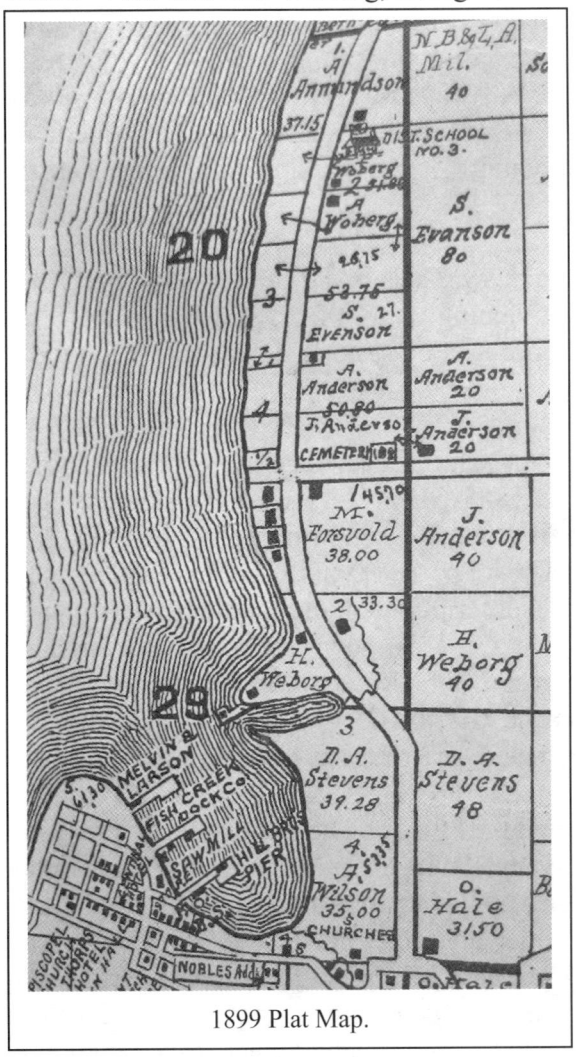

1899 Plat Map.

Increase Claflin had built a cabin at Weborg Point in 1854. Claflin is remembered for be-ing the first white set-tler in Door County having settled at Little Sturgeon Bay in 1835. Claflin moved North to the Weborg Point site after his not so diplo-matic brother-in-law created problems by not trading fairly with Indians at Little Stur-geon Bay. A plaque citing the location of the cabin was unveiled by the Door County Historical Society on Sunday, September 12, 1954 and can be found today in the shelter building at Weborg Point.

The ownership of this piece of property is an interesting story having been recorded by Victoria Dirst, doing an archeological survey in the area. This survey detailed the history of the 33 acres at Weborg Point. John Fitzgerald was the first recorded owner of the property in 1850.

It was next purchased by John Reynolds in 1852 and then by Increase and Mary Claflin in 1855. Mary Claflin sold 31 acres of the land to Andrew Wiberg for $300 in 1865. But for $5, Mary retained the cemetery located on the property consisting of one square rod (an area 16 ½ feet square) known as "Claflin burreing ground." It is interesting to note there were different ways of spelling Weborg as well as "burying" in 1865. Andrew passed the land on to Ole Wiberg in 1870. It stayed in the family until Henry Wiborg sold it to the state in 1909.

There were subdivisions of this property sold to Carl Lundberg, the Thorps and the Larsons explaining many of the old log cabins that used to be located along Shore Road just north of Weborg Point indicated by the small black squares on the map.

There were four graves in the Claflin cemetery in 1865 with burial dates ranging from 1850 to 1865 when Mary Claflin made arrangements to retain ownership of the square rod of property. In 1902, Asa and Roy Thorp purchased a small piece of land from the Lundbergs to expand the cemetery. The description of this addition starts with, "Beginning at a Norway pine . . . " So now you know why this historic cemetery directly across Shore Road from the Weborg Point Campground is known as the Claflin-Thorp cemetery and why the actual boundaries of the cemetery may be hard to determine!

The park board had estimated the land for The Park could be obtained for $20 an acre on the average which for 3800 acres would total $76,000; close to the original appropriation of $75,000. But "average" can be deceiving. Engelbert Folda got $5,000 for his 38 acre Horseshoe Island, or $132 per acre. If the original appropriation was not to be exceeded, much land would need to be acquired for less than $20 an acre. The tactics used to pressure land owners to accept a low price created much controversy. Some people were very happy to receive $20 an acre or less for land they considered worthless. Others were not so happy.

An article titled "The Rights of State Park Property Owners" in the September 9, 1909 Door County Advocate reported on the efforts to acquire property for The Park. "Standing at the foot of Eagle Bluff lighthouse, a certain member of the park board looked out over the proposed park tract and said to the lighthouse keeper, Captain Wm. Duclon, and others, 'I shall buy or condemn this park tract, and I shall pay at the rate of not more than $5 to $8 per acre'." The article went on to state that much of the land, particularly that along the stage road that formed the southern boundary of The Park was only worth $5 to $10 an acre, but that other areas of The Park contained good farm land and was worth much more. "Sunset Cliff (Sven's Bluff), with 37 acres, owned by A. Amondsen, has for three years been held at $3,000, and just before the park board came up, Miss Elwell, later Mrs. Stephenson, was on the point of buying it at that figure. Finally, Mr. Pinney, an agent for the park board, with threats of his famous assessment roll, beat the price down to $2,500."

Hjalmar Holand was especially upset at the tactics used to secure options on the land including Mr. Pinney's use of the tax assessment role to set a low purchase price. Holand, a long time resident of Ephraim, renowned Door County historian and civic leader, owned land just west of Eagle Bluff. Then as now, the assessed value of property for tax purposes may not reflect the market value of the property. In a letter published in the Door County Advocate of March 18, 1909, Mr. Holand said, "The famous assessment role is the chief reliance of the ponderous Mr. Pinney. He swung it threateningly over the head of the bewildered farmer whose only offense was that he would not part with his home, and he brandished it before the eyes of the terrified housewife in the modest little kitchen."

But Mr. Pinney prevailed, and most of the land designated for The Park, with the exception of a few hundred acres, was acquired by 1914. A 1914 plat map shows only eight properties, comprising about 300 acres, not under ownership by the state. Some that gave up their land were given "life leases" so they could remain on the property for the rest of their lives.

Hjalmar Holand was opposed to The Park project. In his 1917 History of Door County Wisconsin, Holand wrote, "The establishment of this park has so far been a poor business investment for Door County and particularly for the Town of Gibraltar. This vast tract which now pays no taxes would with its eight miles of the best water front in the county yield several thousand dollars annually in taxes if open for settlement." But Holand did reserve some guarded optimism for the future. ". . . with the protection of the State, Peninsula Park may in the future become an object of pilgrimage to distant nature worshipers."

Holand's "sour grapes" attitude can easily be understood. Holand lost title to 56 acres of prime real estate. Stand today at the Eagle Panorama and look out over the waters of Green Bay toward Horseshoe Island. This land, all the way down to the shoreline, was once owned by Mr. Holand. He had good reason to be upset. His attitude did change in a few years. What was once a great disappointment became an opportunity. The establishment of The Park gave Holand and the Men's Club in Ephraim an opportunity to get state funds to make badly needed improvements in The Park boundary road between Fish Creek and Ephraim. Holand also became a promoter of the golf links established in The Park in 1921. Later on, Mr. Holand initiated a project to establish a memorial pole to honor the Native Americans and early white settlers in Door County which was erected at the golf course in 1927. History has proven that Mr. Holand did change his attitude about The Park.

Had The Park not been established in 1909, the residents of Fish Creek and Ephraim may be looking at bluffs sprouting condominiums instead of trees. The Eagle Bluff Stone Company that owned most of Eagle Bluff may have continued mining limestone at this site until it became a scar on the land. Acquiring land for The Park was not always a perfect process. But it resulted in preserving 3,800 acres of paradise called Peninsula State Park which is now the jewel of the Wisconsin State Park System.

Six

Al Doolittle

In a letter to the Door County Advocate of January 28, 1909 Holand argued that without land owners present to maintain the primitive roads in The Park, these roads would wash out and become impossible to travel. He argued that without people living on the farms in The Park, forest fires would become a problem because there would be no one to spot the fires and put them out before they spread. Holand predicted the area would revert to the wild and become a breeding ground for wolves that attacked sheep on area farms. Holand questioned where people would stay that came to enjoy The Park since all the accommodations in Fish Creek and Ephraim were filled to capacity each summer. He lamented the fact that more hotels could not be built along the shore in The Park. In his own words in his letter: ". . . when this promising tract is laid waste; when the woods will stand charred and blackened by frequent forest fires; when the untilled fields will be overgrown with weeds; when the houses where they stopped to visit will stand deserted, broken down and wrecked, the impression will be so dismal that hundreds of our present annual visitors will spend their vacation elsewhere to avoid this dismal sight." What Holand did not anticipate was the arrival of Alfred E. Doolittle in 1913 as the first superintendent of The Park.

Al Doolittle was a promoter. But most important, like John Nolan, he had a vision. Al Doolittle prevented The Park from becoming the "dismal" place Holand predicted.

Ed Schreiber remembered Doolittle as being an outspoken man who was very forceful with his ideas. Schreiber said Doolittle often went beyond what his budget allowed, but always, somehow, he got the project done. Ed Schreiber remembered Doolittle as being quite a character: "If you ever asked him how he was, he was always chewing on a cigar, he would answer, 'never better, never better.' That was his stock answer."

The Doolittles had seven children. When they moved to The Park in 1913, the family lived in a small house that proved way too small for the size of the family. The problem was solved in 1914 by moving a five bedroom home from elsewhere in The Park to the site where the superintendents' house is now located. This house, with quite a few modifications, is the underlying structure that makes up the present day superintendents' house.

Dorothy Halverson told me a story about the superintendents' house. When the new house was being set on its foundations, Lettie Doolittle wanted it placed so she had a view of the water. Al had the house set so Lettie had to be standing at the kitchen sink to see the water!

In 1913, major roads in the county were difficult to travel. The "roads" in The Park were worse. Gerhard Miller related a story about the difficulty of early automobile travel in the county. His father bought their first Ford in 1914. He set out with Gerhard and his brother to take a trip around northern Door County. His mother packed some food including a canning jar full of milk. By noon of the first day, they had traveled all the way from Sturgeon Bay to Egg Harbor! When they stopped for lunch, they discovered the bouncing Ford had churned the milk. The quart jar had globules of butter floating on top! At the end of the first day, they had traveled all the way to Ephraim. It took two more days to complete their excursion of the county.

Roads were a problem. One of the first things Al Doolittle did was to set about improving the roads in The Park. The Park roads that existed in 1913 were vastly different from what you find today.

Gravel to improve existing roads and build new ones was dug from the ground in the area east of Shore Road and south of Mengelberg Lane.   Later on, the resultant hole became The Park garbage dump where we could always go in the evening to watch raccoons and even once in awhile, a porcupine routing through the garbage. In the picture on the next page, my nephew, Keith and my father have found a porcupine at the old park dump.

My father at old park dump with his grandson Keith Johnson.
Porcupine highlighted for identification.

The dump is mostly filled and is now only a small depression you can easily identify from the bike trail. Today, instead of holding garbage, it is used by The Park for storing sand, gravel and mulch.

Doolittle laid out the plan for The Park roads we still drive on today. Some of the early roads in The Park have been abandoned and now form parts of the mountain bike trails.

Two observation towers were built utilizing trees cut in The Park in 1914. One, a 45 foot high tower was located at Svens Bluff. A larger tower with a height of 75 feet was built at Eagle Bluff. Jay Doolittle recalls being assigned to Eagle Tower for a few days one summer when it was particularly dry. But the function of the towers was not really for fire protection purposes. Al Doolittle was a promoter. Building an observation tower to be used to prevent forest fires would be seen as a worthwhile project by the Wisconsin Conservation Commission. But more importantly, the towers became a feature of The Park which served to draw visitors. I hardly ever pass Eagle

Tower when there is not at least one person making the climb to the top. Everyone likes to climb a tower!

The Original Eagle Tower.
Photo, Peninsula State Park.

Three different trees were stacked, one upon the other at each corner of the tower. Each pole only spanned the distance between the platforms. This necessitated the use of guy wires, not visible in this picture, securely anchored into the ground at a distance from the tower to help stabilize the structure. The original tower was taken down in 1932 and the present day tower was built at the same location. The present tower was built from very tall trees imported from Washington State allowing each corner to be constructed from just one pole. The pole in the center of the tower was erected first, and then the four corner poles were raised using the center pole for support. This work was performed by a private contractor. But even with these five solid trees for support, the current tower will sway a bit in the wind and I sometimes wish it had guy wires! If it's windy, I usually just hurry back down those 109 stairs. The center support has been repaired throughout the years with the addition of new sections.

The tower at Sven's Bluff was removed in 1947 when the wood rotted making it unsafe. It was not replaced because the overlook at this location provided a good view without the necessity of the additional elevation provided by a tower.

In 1917, the Wisconsin Conservation Commission developed a working plan for the forest lands of Peninsula State Park. The commission reported The Park was well supplied with roads and would become more so, when a road from the lighthouse going around the edge of Welcker's Point was completed. Two of the features mentioned in the Conservation Commission report were the lookout towers. "From these, signs of fire can be seen at any point on this park." The commission also cited the work that had been done to run seven miles of telephone line connecting the villages of Fish Creek and Ephraim with the superintendent's house, the tower at Sven's Bluff, and the lighthouse. The commission noted most of The Park had been stripped of its virgin timber years ago and the land was now covered with second growth trees. About one-quarter of the land had been cleared for farming use. A survey was conducted of the timber in The Park and plans established for planting additional trees and harvesting some of the existing timber. A sawmill located just off Middle Road operated from 1920 until 1961 providing lumber for Peninsula State Park and other parks in the state park system.

Doolittle had already made use of one house located in The Park by turning it into his residence. Other buildings in the park remained occupied by their original owners, or others, who rented or leased them from The Park. This was particularly true of the numerous cabins located along the west Shore Road in The Park.

Bill Carlson and his brother, both fishermen, continued to live in their cabin just north of Weborg Point. Bill Carlson's housekeeper, Gertrude Lund, continued to live in the house after Bill Carlson died and the property reverted to ownership by the state.

Miss Keuchler leased a cabin at Sven's Bluff, living there all year. She had a grand piano, a good voice and gave music lessons. Ed Schreiber took some lessons from her. Miss Keuchler was a great annoyance to park personnel because she was always getting her auto-mobile stuck on The Park roads.

Miss Gatter lived at and ran what could be called a little gift shop called the Owls Nest just back from Shore Road, close to Camp Mee-nahga. The cabin was constructed in 1922 around a cooper's fire-place, the only thing left standing when Even Nelson's cooperage was destroyed by fire some time before 1900. A cooperage was a place where wood barrels were made. Fishing was a primary means of making a living in 1852 when Nelson built the cooperage. Nelson had a good business making barrels for shipping fish to markets out-side Door County. Miss Gatter built Owls Nest around Nelson's old fireplace using logs salvaged from a barn located on Sven's Bluff.

The cabin Lilia and Lydia Dyer occupied on Shore Road.
Now located at The Ridges Sanctuary.

Lilia and Lydia Dyer occupied a cabin on Shore Road just beyond where The Park office is located today. The Dyers were retired school teachers from St. Louis and loved to entertain. Neither lady drove an automobile. The residents of Cottage Row in Fish Creek would send their chauffeurs to transport the ladies to parties. Fortunately, the Dyer cottage was not razed, but transported to the Ridges Sanctuary in Baileys Harbor where it can still be seen today.

The Bach family from Evanston, Illinois occupied a cabin on the shore close to Mengelberg Lane. The Kodanko family operated a farm on Middle Road. The Kodanko children walked over two miles to school each day even in the winter.

A story contained in "Fish Creek - The Summertime," a collection of memoirs, is told by Linda Neeck Smith who spent many summers at Welcker's resort. Linda recalled a favorite pastime of hiking a trail past Devil's Pulpit. Devil's Pulpit is a geologic feature which can be seen today off a winter cross country ski trail east of The Park office. Linda recalls the Welckers packing a lunch for the hike and the hikers investigating old cabins, especially a log cabin at Tennison Bay that had Swedish newspapers from 1860 stuffed in the ceiling for insulation.

Gerhard Miller remembers camping at Nicolet Bay. Later, his father rebuilt an old fisherman's cabin located on Tennison Bay just south of the lighthouse. Doolittle told Gerhard's father he could rebuild the dilapidated cabin but they had to use only the original materials they found at the site; they could use no new lumber. Gerhard and his father were able to reconstruct a small cabin with two bunks, a table and a window overlooking Tennison Bay.

The Fitzgeralds had a cabin just a bit further up the road toward the lighthouse. Gerhard remembered Friday evening bonfires with the Fitzgeralds. Gerhard's mother would make up a pot of beans, seal the lid with some dough and Gerhard would place the pot in a hole he dug near the bonfire. When the fire burned down, Gerhard would rake the coals into the hole with the bean pot and cover everything with dirt. The next day, they enjoyed a delicious treat Gerhard called "bean hole beans."

Gerhard's father had the cabin for about ten years until he learned The Park was going to eventually require all these old cabins be demolished.   Gerhard's father sold the place to Cornelius Harrington, the Superintendent of State Forests and Parks.   Harrington had the cabin for a few years before it was eventually torn down.

Many of the old houses and cabins were deserted.   But others were occupied by those living out their life lease or by those who rented or leased the buildings providing needed income for The Park.   For the most part, they did not stand deserted as Holand once predicted.   Al Doolittle was following his vision for slowly evolving the old homesteads into a state park.

But camping is what really brought people to The Park.   The 1921 visitors guide listed the following number of lots that had been laid out along the shore of The Park and could be leased for camping:

Thirty-two lots at Eagle Spring near Ephraim. Later called Crystal Springs, this campground closed in 1950.   Twenty lots at Shanty Bay now called Nicolet Bay.   The Shanty Bay name came from the "shanties" people used to build for the summer. Eleven lots near Fish Creek.   Today we know this campground as Weborg Point.

The "lots" could be leased for fifty cents a week or $5.00 for the season.   In addition each lot lessee had to make a $5.00 deposit with the park superintendent.   If you left your lot in a good clean and sanitary condition, your $5.00 was refunded.   If not, the park superintendent would use your deposit to pay for the work necessary to clean up your site.

Today, there are 188 sites at Nicolet Bay, 189 at Tennison Bay, 81 at Welcker's Point, and 12 at Weborg Point; 470 total.   Camping has been, and still is, the largest activity drawing people to The Park.

Seven

Horseshoe Island

As a child camping in The Park in the 1950s, I would often go to Horseshoe Island to explore. I discovered the old ice house back in the woods. I knew the stories about Jean Nicolet visiting the area in 1634 and that perhaps he had also visited this island. I imagined this ice house as having been built by Nicolet! Never mind the reality that Nicolet had stayed in this area no more than two weeks and that his visit was made in the summer. I also conveniently ignored that the ice house was made of concrete. There is nothing more adventurous than a child's imagination.

Carol and I sitting with nephews Kevin and Keith Johnson
on the stone patio on Horseshoe Island in 1968.

Whenever I went to the island, I would pull our boat up on the shore at a place where there was a large patio made of cobblestones expertly set into concrete. These were the finest cobblestones I had seen anywhere in Door County including those at the famed Schoolhouse Beach on Washington Island.

Who had built this wonderful patio? What had been here many years ago? It was a mystery I needed to unravel.

Increase Claflin named the island Eagle Island because he found an eagle nest here. The name Horseshoe Island originated from the island's shape; a deep natural harbor on the south side gives it the unmistakable shape of a horseshoe. Horseshoe Island is the name used today.

I knew that Ole Larson had come to the Island in 1852 looking for a good spot to fish. Reportedly, Larson traded a small quantity of tobacco for the island. The fishing was good, but so was the business of supplying wood for the steamer from Buffalo, New York that made a weekly run to Green Bay. Ole stripped the Island clean of trees in just a couple years and then moved his home across Nicolet Bay where a plaque close to campsite 752 marks the spot.

But fisherman, lumberman and farmer Ole Larson would never have built the beautiful stone patio I was standing on. The unraveling of the mystery came in 1998 when I purchased a copy of the book, "Horseshoe Island, The Folda Years," written by Stanford H. Sholem.

There were many people who have owned Horseshoe Island since Ole Larson had his cabin there. In 1882 the county treasurer bought the island for $18.46 in back taxes. Frank Folda, a banker from Nebraska, bought the Island in 1888 for $500. Frank died in 1892 leaving all his property to his children, Engelbert and Martha.

In 1909 when the state was beginning to acquire land for a state park, Horseshoe Island was to become part of that park. Engelbert Folda, like many others who wanted to keep their land, was able to secure a life lease on the property so the family could enjoy it until they died.

Engelbert built a beautiful summer residence on the island called Engelmar. The magnificent stone steps and patio I wondered about were part of the estate.

In the stock market crash of 1929 and the collapse of the banking industry in the years that followed, Folda's bank in Nebraska failed and Folda personally suffered financial collapse. He died in Los Angeles in 1944. Shortly after his death, his wife, Alma, relinquished any remaining life estate rights at Horseshoe Island to the State of Wisconsin for $850.

The natural harbor at the island often contained yachts belonging to friends of the Folda's or simply vessels seeking shelter from a storm. Magnificent boats have long used this harbor as a place of shelter. Back in the 1950s, before there was a time limit on camping in The Park, the Krubsack family camped all summer at Nicolet Bay. Gary Krubsack and I became friends and spent much time on Horseshoe Island. One day we got the surprise of our lives as we entered the harbor. Tucked back into the west corner of the harbor was the yacht Utopia, a sixty-five foot schooner owned by Fred Peterson, chairman of the Sturgeon Bay shipbuilding firm bearing his name. The Utopia carried 2,500 square feet of sail, and every bit of that sail was hoisted that day. It had been raining. The Utopia was tied up at Horseshoe to dry out her sails. Gary told me the Utopia had sailed around the world. Indeed, Fred Peterson, in his sixty-second year, hoisted anchor at Sturgeon Bay in 1956, took the Utopia down the Mississippi River and spent three years sailing around the world crossing three oceans and ten seas along the way. Folda's Engelmar was gone. Many of the fine yachts that once filled this natural harbor only exist as photographs in someone's prized album. But on that day, Gary and I saw a magnificent sailboat anchored in a magnificent harbor.

Stanford H. Sholem's book, "Horseshoe Island, The Folda Years," is a must read for anyone interested not only in the history of this 40 acre island, but for a glimpse into the social times of the early 1900s. Summer estates like Engelmar provided extraordinary settings for a family and their guests to enjoy a life style that brings back images from F. Scott Fitzgerald's writings. This book also tells the story of a man with great integrity, who did everything he could to help repay the people who had lost money in his bank. It brings joy to the heart as you read it and a tear to your eye at the end.

You must search today for what little remains now of the stone steps and the patio.

Entropy - the process, where things that have been built by man or by nature, eventually degrade back to their original state.

The stone patio and steps of Engelmar on Horseshoe Island.

And where did those perfect cobblestones come from? That's a mystery you will have to unravel by reading Sholem's book.

Eight

The Lighthouse

Henry Stanley, keeper, climbed the circular staircase to the lantern room on the night of October 15, 1868 and lit the oil fired lamp. For the first time, the three and one-half order Fresnel lens, focused light from the lamp out over the waters of Green Bay. The light could be seen for fifteen miles in clear weather.

Increasing maritime traffic in 1860, passing through the channel located between the Strawberry Islands and the mainland, caused the Federal Lighthouse Board to request a lighthouse be constructed on Eagle Bluff north of Fish Creek. The city of Green Bay was booming with 35 saw mills. Smaller villages on the shores of Green Bay were shipping barrels of fish to market. Schooner and steamer traffic required navigation aids to assure safe passage as they traveled up and down the bay. Twelve thousand dollars was appropriated in 1866 for construction of the Eagle Bluff light. The Eagle Bluff light and the one on Chambers Island were constructed in 1868. The Eagle Bluff light and the Chambers Island light were virtual twins with the exception of the light tower. The tower at the Eagle Bluff light is square; the one at Chambers Island is octagonal. This difference is called a "day mark," a feature designed to allow a visual distinction to be made between similar navigation aids. The light at Cana Island went into operation a year later.

Henry Stanley was transferred from Eagle Bluff to the Sherwood Point light at Sturgeon Bay in 1883. William Duclon assumed the duties of "keeper" on September 20 of that year. William was a civil war veteran, wounded in the battle of Gettysburg, and honorably discharged in 1864. He had served at two other lighthouses before coming to Eagle Bluff. Many lighthouse keepers were civil war veterans. Anyone applying for lighthouse duty had to pass the light keeper's exam to become qualified, but veterans were given preferential treatment.

William Duclon and his wife Julia had seven sons, the youngest being one year old when they moved into their new quarters at Eagle Bluff. What a place to raise seven boys! The boys fished and swam in the bay. They hunted small game and deer right out their back door. They constructed ice boats and skimmed over the frozen water in the winter. The boys carried water from the bay, up the bluff, until a well was drilled through the rock utilizing real "horse power," actual horses to turn the drill, in the late 1800s. Now the boys didn't have to climb stairs to supply water for their needs, but they did have to work a pump handle. Julia Duclon was interested in music and taught the boys how to play the piano and other instruments. The Duclon boys provided lively music for area dances.

The life of a keeper was regimented. Strict government regulations governed a keeper's day. Uniforms called "dress" were worn. Inspections of the lighthouse were made on a surprise basis and everything had to be in perfect order. But the Duclon boys were good at spotting boats approaching the small dock at the base of the bluff and could often sound the alarm allowing last minute preparations to be completed before the inspector set foot on the shore. The long climb up a flight of stairs ascending the bluff gave everyone a little more time!

The light was converted from oil to kerosene in the late 1800s. Wicks and lard oil were stored in a small closet on the second floor, close to the spiral stairs leading up the tower. But frequent lightening strikes to the tower made storing the volatile kerosene somewhere else sound like a good idea! A small brick building was constructed a safe distance away from the lighthouse for this purpose. The building exists today and can still be seen close to the edge of the bluff south of the lighthouse

A keeper's life was not all work and regulations. A fleet of government operated tenders serviced the lighthouses and delivered traveling libraries of books for reading. Visitors often came to the lights. The keeper and their families were expected to show them good hospitality.

William Duclon retired in 1918 after 35 years service at Eagle Bluff and 45 years duty in the Light Keeping Service. He didn't move far. The Duclons chose Fish Creek for their retirement home.

Peter Coughlin, the next and final keeper at Eagle Bluff, arrived to assume duties at the same time a smaller fifth order Fresnel lens was installed. A three and one-half order Fresnel lens was forty inches high and weighed close to 1,000 pounds. A fifth order lens was about half that height and weighed about 300 pounds. Although the new lens was smaller than the original, the light source had been improved substantially from the original oil fired lamp.

Peter Coughlin tended the light until it was automated in 1926 with the installation of acetylene light. On September 15, 1926, Peter Coughlin made the last entry in his log. I hope he placed the distinguished title of "Keeper" after his name. Today the light is still an active navigation aid utilizing solar power.

The lighthouse sat vacant until 1936 when it was leased to The Park. Even then, it remained mostly vacant except for "little deals" that Cornelius Harrington arranged for employees of the Wisconsin Conservation Department. Harrington was the Superintendent of State Forests and Parks in Wisconsin. As such, he was now "keeper of the lighthouse" even though the light in the tower was maintained by the Coast Guard. Harrington often allowed conservation department personnel to stay at the lighthouse. Mary Ellen Smith recorded an entry in the memory book at the Nature Center related to such an experience. She remembered staying at the lighthouse for a week in the 1950s. Her father was a supervisor with the Wisconsin Conservation Department. What a way to give out nice rewards to department personnel. I would not hesitate to select a night at Eagle Bluff over a night in the Lincoln Bedroom at the White House if I were given a chance.

Years passed. The lighthouse was deteriorating. Around 1960, the Door County Historical Society was looking for an important landmark to restore and then be used to display historic pieces in their collection. Many places were considered. Lowell Hanson, park superintendent at the time, suggested Eagle Bluff Lighthouse. Fortunately for the Eagle Bluff lighthouse, the historical society chose it as their project.

Restoring the lighthouse was no small undertaking. Remember, the Light Keeping Service had performed frequent inspections when the light was tended by a keeper. If the house had to be spotless, what is the best way to eliminate dirt on floors, walls and woodwork that can't be removed with soap and water? Paint is the answer. As part of the restoration, over eighty layers of paint had to be removed from the pine woodwork.

Lowell Hanson found the original plans for the lighthouse. The work, involving thousands of hours by historical society volunteers, restored and then furnished Eagle Bluff Lighthouse according to the period. When you enter the lighthouse today on a guided tour, you will step back over one hundred years in time. These tours impart a sense of what life was like at this wonderful place.

After your tour, take a minute to hike Trail Tramper's Delight which begins across Shore Road from the lighthouse and leads over to Nicolet Bay. The Duclon brothers once owned land on Nicolet Bay, where this trail ends at the edge of the campground. This trail pre-dates the establishment of The Park by many years. Let your imagination wander. You may see and hear seven boys romping down this trail, on their way to and from Nicolet Bay.

Nine

The Golf Course

In 1913, The Ephraim Men's Club requested part of The Park to be set aside for golf links. Doolittle set about to create two golf courses, one on the Evenson farm where Camp Meenahga was later located and another at an old farm near the present day Ephraim park entrance. Some improvements were made at the Ephraim site, but they proved to be "entirely inadequate." After a few years, the Ephraim Men's Club obtained a verbal lease for the links. Good greens were built. As the links became popular, several thousand dollars were raised each summer and the money was used to make improvements. When the links became an assured success, the Wisconsin Conservation Commission revoked the lease and took over management of the golf course.

The above account is based upon information written in a 1932 publication titled "Reminiscences of Twenty Years Activity of a Community Club." The Community Club was the Ephraim Men's Club. This account is probably too biased against the Wisconsin Conservation Commission and too biased in favor of what the Men's Club did. Nevertheless, what began as an idea with the Ephraim Men's Club, did result in the creation of a golf course, the beginnings of which were successfully nurtured by the Ephraim Men's Club. And although it was then managed for years by the State of Wisconsin, it did, under state operation, grow to become a wonderful golf course. The Peninsula Golf Association assumed management of the course and clubhouse in 1981 and today maintains a top notch golf facility and the only golf course, located in a Wisconsin State Park.

Al Doolittle abandoned the Evenson farm site due to the problem of getting water for the greens. But the Ephraim entrance site was developed. By 1921 the course was operational. The Door County Advocate reported on June 3, 1921 that the new golf links, laid out by W. R. Lovekin of Green Bay, would be ready for play in July. The diorama recording at the nature center says, "It functioned with sand greens for the first ten years." By 1931, The Wisconsin Conservation

Commission State Park pamphlet for Peninsula State Park boasted of the excellent 18 hole golf course, carved out of the woods and overlooking the bay. The pamphlet stated the course offered a treat to golfers difficult to duplicate anywhere.

The Ephraim Men's Club established a clubhouse shortly after the course became operational. It was located across the road from the present day clubhouse. This original clubhouse was converted from a granary and included a screened porch to give golfers respite from mosquitoes.

At the time the golf course was built, the highway that formed the southern boundary of the course, curved off to the right as it descended the steep hill into Ephraim. This original section of road still exists as Holand Road beginning just opposite the golf course entrance to The Park. Early autos did not have enough power to go directly up a steep hill so a slight diversion around the hill was required. The highway was realigned to descend the hill directly around 1940. Hole number five on the golf course then became an island bounded by the new route for the highway and Holand Road. Golfers had to cross Highway 42 to play the hole. Imagine doing that today! In the 1960s, the golf course was redesigned and hole number five moved to the north side of the highway.

You can still find interesting historic evidence of the golf course in areas of The Park far removed from the golf course itself. If you walk through the large open field on the north side of Middle Road, just east of the intersection with Hemlock Road, where the old Kodanko farm was located, you will find an area of smooth, flat rock, so perfect; you might imagine it to have been used as a patio covering many acres. Dirt was removed from here to be used in the process of rebuilding the golf course back in the 1960s.

I am not a golfer. But when I mention Peninsula State Park, I get an equal number of responses concerning what a wonderful place it is to camp and what a wonder place it is to golf. Not everyone feels this way. I knew one Door County golfer who used to snort, "You have to be half mountain goat to play Peninsula!" If you are a golfer, and you are at the tee at the eighth hole, looking fifty feet straight down to the green, you will understand this mountain goat statement! Neverthe-less, this golf course is a treasure. In addition to their work maintaining and managing the course, the Peninsula Golf Association has also done much to support non-golf related park projects.

Ten

Camp Meenahga

The sweet corn in our garden always seemed to reach perfection just after we left home to vacation in The Park. This problem was overcome with the help of a neighbor, Ed Dorsey, who flew his own airplane. Ed knew where we camped. He would come in low over the water, roaring over our camp with enough racket to shake the squirrels out of the trees. We knew our sweet corn would arrive in a few minutes at the Ephraim-Fish Creek Airport.

Ed liked to camp and would stay for the weekend. Once, he brought two scuba tanks so we could do some underwater exploring. We filled the tanks with air at the scuba shop in Fish Creek and asked for a good place to dive in The Park. It was suggested we dive off the old stone steps along Shore Road just north of Mengelberg Lane. We were told to descend along the drop-off to where the bottom turned to sand. There we could find old barrel staves by fanning the sand. The staves must have come from Even Nelson's cooperage which had been located just north of this place. Ed and I never recovered any old barrel staves. The temperature of the surface water was in the low sixties, but when we hit the thermal cline at about eight feet the temperature dropped into the low fifties. We did not have wet suits. This was the end of the dive, but not of my questions. Why were those steps there?

Ed Dorsey and I diving at The Park.

Even Nelson could have had a pier in this area to ship out his barrels. But he would certainly not have built an elaborate stone patio, surrounded with a low stone wall including a gazebo and having steps leading down to the water. Something else had been here many years ago. The mystery was further confounded with my knowledge that old tennis courts existed up in the woods across the road from these stone steps. Why would anyone build tennis courts out in the middle of nowhere? Years later, I learned about Camp Meenahga.

In 1916, two widows, Alice Orr Clark and Fannie Woodward Mabley from St. Louis, were looking for a place to establish a summer camp for girls. There were youth camps operating at Sawyer, Wisconsin in the area of the lighthouse at Sherwood Point. The ladies also looked at locations in Peninsula State Park as a possibility. Superintendent

Doolittle, always interested in anything that would help promote his new state park, was enthusiastic about the idea of a girls' camp. The ladies selected the old Evenson farm that had been purchased by The Park a few years earlier. The farm had a barn that could be used as a dining and recreation hall and a cottage for the two ladies. The campers would stay in tents. The ladies named the camp "Meenahga" meaning the blueberry, a word from Longfellow's epic poem, Hiawatha. This name came to mind when the two ladies were looking at a site in the Sawyer area which had an abundance of blueberries. The name also fit perfectly with the set of dishes they acquired from a defunct maritime operation that had a large "M" emblazoned on each piece!

Meenahga was some camp. It had a large riding ring. Horses were leased from area stables and the girls became accomplished riders. There were tennis courts. There was swimming in the bay, canoeing, overnight camping trips to other locations in The Park and of course,

Diving raft at Camp Meenahga.
Photo from the Roy Gauger Collection, Peninsula State Park.

good camp food. Mr. Kodanko, who operated a farm up on Middle Road delivered fresh vegetables to the camp and hauled out camp garbage to feed to his hogs. An eight week camp session cost $350 in 1924. This was no small amount. You could purchase an automobile for what you would spend to send two or three of your daughters to camp for eight weeks at Meenahga. Most of the girls came from well-to-do families in the St. Louis area.

Alice Orr Clark's daughter, Alice Clark Peddle has recorded some interesting stories about camp life in "Fish Creek – The Summertime." One of the favorite places for the girls to go to get ice cream was the Maple Tree Café, now the Summertime in Fish Creek. The girls would purchase a pack of Camel cigarettes supposedly for Mr. Stephenson, the camp master. Of course, the girls smoked the cigarettes themselves! Guests from the Welcker hotel would walk past the camp on Shore Road speaking German. The girls used to imagine they were spies! Remember, World War I did not end until November 11, 1918.

Al Doolittle had salvaged a ship's bell and propeller off an old wreck. Doolittle, being Irish, painted the propeller green and called it a shamrock. It sat on a mantle in the dining room and the ship's bell was used to call the girls to meals.

Duncan Thorp, who grew up in Fish Creek, worked one summer at Camp Meenahga when he was 15. He maintained the tennis courts and did other chores at the camp. One of his duties was getting the mail. All the girl's mail was opened before it was delivered. Any money was removed and placed in the girl's account for safety until they withdrew small amounts for making purchases in town.

Duncan Thorp convinced Roselyn, one of the girls at the camp, to sneak out and go to a dance with him. To do so, Roselyn would need money to bribe her counselor so she would not be reported at bed check time. Duncan delivered Roselyn's mail directly, bypassing the inspection process so Roselyn could secretly accumulate the bribe money.

Everything went well, until the couple returned to camp at 2:30 A.M. to find all the lights on in the office. The counselor, not true to his word, had reported Roselyn missing!

If you have ever been to summer camp, you know how much fun it was and probably delight in the stories you can still recall. The stories about Meenahga could fill volumes. But now, I know exactly what I needed to know. I know why those steps are located along Shore Road and why there are tennis courts in the woods.

Stone Steps along Shore Road at Camp Meenahga
Photo from the Roy Gauger Collection, Peninsula State Park

Eleven

The Fire

The Wisconsin Conservation Commission study of 1917 commented on past management of timber located in The Park. Their survey showed little damage due to fires in the case of trees presently growing in The Park, but that bad fires had swept large areas of The Park in previous times. Blackened and fire scarred tree trunks were cited as evidence.

There was one bad fire in The Park that was documented by Duncan Thorp. Thorp noted that the state had cut much of the valuable timber in the park leaving the woods scattered with harvest debris. A severe drought around 1926 created the potential for a disaster that actually occurred.

The Thorps had a farm across the highway from The Park. One day they spotted smoke from a fire in The Park and quickly plowed a fire break around their farm buildings because of the potential for the fire to cross the road and destroy their farm. Once this precaution was complete, the Thorps joined park personnel and other volunteers from the area to fight the fire in The Park.

Duncan recalls the men fought the fire for weeks. Although they could extinguish the fire, it would flare up again in new places. The earth was so dry and full of cracks that the fire ran underground sustained by burning tree roots. When this underground fire found a place to surface, an old hollow tree for example, it would begin anew requiring the men fight the new fire. The men slept in The Park always on the lookout for new fires. It took a soaking rain to finally eliminate the danger. But there was some good that came from it all. Duncan remembers bumper crops of blackberries that thrived in areas the fire had devastated.

Besides the fire Duncan Thorp recalled, there was a false alarm spread once when pranksters from the Fish Creek Yacht Club decided to yell "Fire!" The story recorded by Bernard Rogers in "Fish Creek -

the Summertime," recalls these pranksters becoming concerned about the growing number of campers in The Park. With the help of a portable loud speaker recently acquired by the Yacht Club for calling sailboat races, the pranksters drove through The Park campgrounds one evening announcing a fire out of control in The Park. They called for everyone to immediately abandon their camps and to report to Wilson's in Ephraim for instructions. The pranksters then settled back to watch a string of headlights headed toward Wilson's.

Twelve

The Memorial Pole

The idea to erect a memorial pole originated with Hjalmar Holand in the late 1920s. With support from the Ephraim Men's Club, the Door County Historical Society, and Superintendent Doolittle, Holand's idea became reality. Holand envisioned a memorial honoring the Potawatomi who occupied the Door Peninsula before the arrival of the first white settlers.

A large pine tree, which had been struck by lightning along the old Owl City Trail close to Eagle Terrace, was selected to become the Memorial Pole. Holand envisioned six "panels" on the pole depicting Native Americans hunting deer, the coming of the missionaries, the arrival of European settlers, the French and English wars, the fur trade, and lastly, the Native Americans being driven from their lands by white settlers. Vida Weborg, still living in her home in The Park, created drawings for each panel based on Holand's ideas.

A woodcarver from Sister Bay offered to do the carving for 50 cents an hour. He died before beginning the task. Charles Lesaar, an artist who summered in a rented cottage on Shore Road in The Park, took up the carving task. Lesaar completed the work in three weeks. Robert Petschneider of Kewaunee, well known for producing religious sculptures, carved the climbing bear perched on the top of the pole. The bear, "Owasse," was revered by both the Potawatomi and Menominee as being a clever and cunning animal. Today, Owasse, from the original memorial pole can be seen at the nature center in The Park.

Dignitaries at the Memorial Pole.
Al Doolittle far left standing next to Cornelius Harrington, Superintendent of Wisconsin State Parks and Forests. Others unknown to the author.
Photo, Wisconsin Historical Society, image ID 38950.

The memorial pole was dedicated on Sunday, August 14, 1927. This was not a small event! Imagine over 5,000 people gathered at the golf course for the dedication. On hand were 32 members of the Potawatomi Tribe from Forest County, Wisconsin. The unveiling was done by Chief Simon Kahquados. At the unveiling, Chief Kahquados said, "We have never looked for any honor from the white people and we have not received any. We are therefore grateful that there are men who look with respect upon our fathers and have raised this pole as a visible sign." The Potawatomi adopted Hjalmar Holand into their tribe. The Potawatomi were extremely poor. Adopting Holand into their tribe was a meaningful and yet affordable way for them to show their appreciation. Chief Kahquados walked up to Holand, shook his hand and proclaimed him Chief Kahgegishkong. Holand was touched by the chief's words. He smiled and said, "Mewish" the Potawatomi word meaning "Thank you."

Chief Simon Kahquados at the Potawatomi Reservation,
Forest County, Wisconsin.
Photo, Wisconsin Historical Society, image ID 38943.

Later in the day, the Potawatomi put on a great display of Native American dancing. Harold Holand, Hjalmar's son, recalls the unforgettable memory of the sound of the tom-toms beating long into the night. All the others who had attended the ceremony earlier had long since retired to bed.

Before Chief Kahquados returned to the Forest County reservation, Holand asked him if he would like to be buried by the memorial pole. Kahquados accepted the offer.

Cars parked on the golf course for the burial of
Chief Simon Kahquados
May 30 – 31, 1931.
Photo, Wisconsin Historical Society, image ID 38949.

Chief Kahquados died in November, 1930. Holand arranged to delay the final burial until the next year when more people would likely attend the ceremony. The Chief was buried next to the memorial pole as part of a two day ceremony in May, 1931. More than 30 Potawatomi came for the ceremony. As the Potawatomi did a few years earlier when the memorial pole was first dedicated, they remained to dance and pay tribute to their Chief, late into the night and long after the others who had attended the ceremony earlier, had gone home.

Entropy - the process, where things that have been built by man or by nature, eventually degrade back to their original state.

By the late 1960's, the memorial pole carved by Charles Lesaar was rotting and needed to be replaced. Adlai Hardin, a renowned sculptor and part-time resident of Ephraim, did the carving of the new memorial pole in the shed alongside the Anderson Store in Ephraim. This pole included the same panels as the original with the addition of a seventh dedicated to the Menominee. Roy Oshkosh, Chief of the Menominee, was asked by Adlai Hardin for suggestions for an additional panel. Chief Roy Oshkosh resided in Egg Harbor. For many years, Roy and his Owassie Dancers presented weekly powwows featuring Indian customs, lore and dancing at an amphitheatre that seated 600 people located at the base of the hill as you come into Egg Harbor from the south. Roy picked a feather design from a centuries-old pair of buckskin leggings. The seventh memorial pole panel representing the Menominee was an appropriate addition to the new monument.

There was some controversy concerning the location for the new pole. The board of directors of the Ephraim Foundation had initiated the project to replace the deteriorated pole. The directors, working with state representatives, had decided to place the new pole directly across Highway 42 from the golf course. The site selected was in the triangle where old hole number five of the golf course had once been located. The reason for this decision had some validity. To view the memorial pole at its original location, people had to walk across the golf course which is permitted only during non-golfing hours. The site across the highway would eliminate this restriction and allow ample parking for those wishing to view the pole. The state planned to landscape the area with a backdrop of evergreens and to provide lighting for the pole.

Word of this decision got out and over 500 people signed petitions requesting the new memorial pole be placed at the site of the original pole, in the vicinity of the gravesite of Chief Kahquados. This is where you will find it today. Jane Shea, writing about this controversy in the July 31, 1969 issue of the Door County Advocate included this wonderful old Indian legend, "He who puts ear to the ground, hears the beat of many drums."

The new memorial pole was set in place in July of 1970 and dedicated on September 12 of that year. Twenty-nine years earlier, on September 12, 1941, a Door County Advocate obituary reported that Charles Lesaar, 57 years old, carver of the original memorial pole, had taken his own life by drowning off the shore of his cottage in Peninsula State Park. Gerhard Miller recalled Charles Lesaar as being a good painter. This is quite a compliment coming from this great Door County artist. However, Lesaar will probably be remembered more for the work he did carving the original memorial pole, than he will for his paintings.

In 1994, the memorial pole was repainted and its life extended with restoration work. Remember, visits to the memorial pole and the grave of Chief Simon Kahquados are permitted only during non-golfing hours. But if you are passing the golf course on a quiet evening, after the golfers have gone, a walk to the pole is a wonderful experience. As you stand by the rock containing the Kahquados memorial plaque, listen to the wind passing through the small grove of pine trees and reflect on the significance of the stories told by the memorial panels.

Here in Peninsula State Park, stands a memorial pole that serves to honor two great Native American Nations.

Thirteen

The CCC Camp

The government description was: Project number SP-10, company No. 3648, established August 12, 1935. Nearest railroad – Sturgeon Bay. Served by post office – Fish Creek. Disbanded June 30, 1937.

Giving work in The Park to unemployed men was not new. The Depression was causing severe financial hardships due to the lack of work. Federal, state and even local agencies were trying to help the unemployed by hiring them for public works projects. In November 1933, the Door County Advocate reported 25 men were being given work at Peninsula State Park under the supervision of Superintendent Doolittle as part of a federal-state relief program. In March of 1934, Doolittle had men working under the Civil Works Administration clearing brush in The Park and also building a 300 foot long dock at Weborg Point to create a natural harbor for small yachts. If time permitted, Doolittle wanted to use the men to extend the dock at Nicolet Bay before the ice went out.

The Civilian Conservation Corps, created in March of 1933 was sometimes called Roosevelt's tree army. The CCC employed over three million young men and planted three billion trees in just nine years, giving needed jobs to America's youth during the Depression. These young men were paid $30 a month, $25 of which was sent home to their families. But the CCC did a lot more than just plant trees.

Cornelius Harrington, Superintendent of Forests and Parks for the Wisconsin State Conservation Department, applied to the Federal Government in February of 1935 to have a CCC camp established at Peninsula State Park. The camp, to be located on the ridge north of Gibraltar High School, was approved in May. Planned work included removing brush, creating fire lanes and trails, building a machine shop and garage for park equipment, and building a ski jump and to-boggan slide in the park.

In August of 1935, ninety men, living in temporary tents, began the construction of Camp Peninsula. The work was done by September and CCC boys were busy collecting field stones to be used in the construction of a machine shop and garage. Soon, there were 200 people living at the camp.

But the seeds for future trouble were being planted. Kenneth Greaves, a landscape architect, and William Bernhard, building architect, were developing projects for The Park under the direction of G. H. Nickell of the National Park Service. The CCC camp itself was run by two Army Lieutenants. Some of the ideas for The Park, envisioned by the CCC, did not resonate with Al Doolittle. Remember how Ed Schreiber described Al Doolittle. "Al Doolittle was an outspoken man who was very forceful with his ideas." Resentment against the camp began to grow, not just with Mr. Doolittle, but with others in the area.

The Gibraltar Men's Club passed a resolution in March of 1936 critical of how the National Park Service was contemplating the development of Peninsula State Park with the assistance of the CCC camp. The resolution expressed the fear that radical changes were being proposed. One of the changes cited was the establishment of a single entrance to The Park located between Fish Creek and Ephraim with a sentry posted to collect admission fees. Doolittle was not against camping fees, but he was very much opposed to entrance fees. Other changes involved the abandonment of some roads. Remember, these roads were laid out and built by Mr. Doolittle with no small effort. The overall fear expressed by the Men's Club resolution was that outsiders were going to take charge of the supervision of The Park.

It was not just the Gibraltar Men's Club that expressed concern. An editorial in the Door County Advocate in March of 1936 also criticized federal interference at The Park. By May, the County Board voted unanimously to support removal of the camp.

Robert Fechner, the Washington D.C. Director of the CCC camps, sent William Hannon to investigate the situation in May, 1936. Hannon stated that this was the first time a request had been made to remove a CCC camp. Hannon listened to those critical of what the

CCC was doing. He also found considerable sentiment in favor of retaining the camp. But he also reported there was no desire to retain the camp in Peninsula if there are good substantial reasons for its removal.

It appears there was some remorse following Hannon's report. A group of citizens and businesspeople from Sturgeon Bay petitioned Robert Fechner to conduct a more complete investigation before any action was taken concerning the closing of Camp Peninsula. Work did continue over the winter, but in June of 1937, the camp was disbanded. CCC buildings had a modular design allowing them to be moved and utilized at other locations. You won't find much evidence of the camp itself in The Park today.

But you will find evidence of the camp by what it accomplished in The Park. Thirteen miles of trails had been constructed. A stone bath house at Nicolet Bay, no longer existing, had been built. The beautiful stonework you see today at Eagle Panorama was a CCC project. The CCC has left its mark on The Park and it was good.

Besides the building projects, the CCC also eradicated acres of poison ivy from The Park. Bips Linn Murray remembered coming to Fish Creek in 1913 when only five years old. Murray recalls there was a wonderful beach at Shanty Bay, now called Nicolet Bay, and that his family often went to this place to swim and have picnics. There was only one problem; you had to get through a huge patch of poison ivy to get to the beach! Today, of course, you can enjoy Nicolet Bay with only a "little threat" from the poison ivy, thanks in part, to the efforts of the CCC.

Fourteen

The Game Farm

Becky Loper wrote in The Park memory book, "I remember riding our bikes up to Eagle Tower. It took us an hour to get up and about 10 minutes to get down." Old timers will tell you the hill that Becky had to ascend to get to the tower was called Game Farm Hill because of the state game farm that used to be located close to the foot of the hill where the group camps are today.

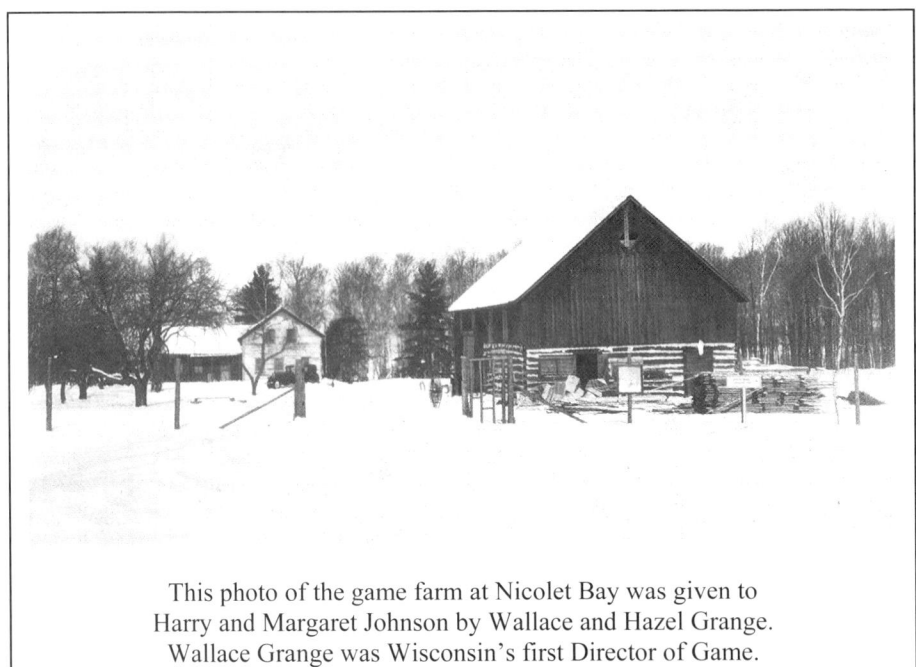

This photo of the game farm at Nicolet Bay was given to
Harry and Margaret Johnson by Wallace and Hazel Grange.
Wallace Grange was Wisconsin's first Director of Game.
Harry Johnson was the first game farm manager.
Photo supplied by Carl Johnson, Harry Johnson's son.

The game farm was a BIG operation. A State Park pamphlet from 1931 invited visitors to the game farm where they could see thousands of ring-necked pheasants and other kinds of fowl including wild American turkeys, Hungarian partridge, sharp-tailed grouse, quail, and several kinds of ducks. The game farm also operated a zoo where birds, animals, and reptiles native to the area could be seen.

A few black bears were included in the zoo. Once, the bears got out creating quite a stir in The Park. Carl Anderson operated a greenhouse on Middle Road throughout the time the game farm operated in The Park. One bear climbed on top of Carl Anderson's greenhouse and crashed down through the glass. I knew Carl Anderson. Nothing would bother Carl very much, but I can imagine there was some excitement with a bear running around his greenhouse.

The game farm operated in The Park from 1928 to 1934 when it was moved to Poynette. Some say the farm was closed because winters in the area were not conducive to raising large numbers of birds. Others say the reasons for moving the farm to Poynette were purely political. While hiking Eagle Trail on a New Year's day some years ago, with the wind really whipping in from the north, I could have been convinced winter weather was the reason for closing the farm. However, politics would probably be the logical conclusion.

The game farm employed a lot of people. Ed Schreiber said the loss of the farm was a great blow to the economy in the area. As you puff and pant going up the hill on Shore Road to Eagle Tower, stop along the way to peer over the edge of the wall along the road and marvel at the stone work in the retaining wall supporting the road. At the top, stop once again to catch your breath. Look back toward the group camp area. Imagine some black bears running through the woods reveling in their newly found freedom.

Fifteen

The Prohibition

In 1920, the eighteenth amendment to our constitution prohibited the manufacture, sale, and transport of alcohol. For thirteen years, this prohibition was the law of the land. The Park was no exception. A park visitor's guide from 1926 clearly stated, "THE PROHIBITION relating to intoxicating liquors on the grounds must be strictly observed by campers and cottagers." The amendment was repealed on December 5, 1933. You still can't purchase alcohol in Ephraim, but I prefer a good chocolate soda at Wilson's anyway!

There were two taverns in The Park at one time. Alfon Jensen opened a tavern on Highland Road in The Park, shortly after prohibition ended. His cousin, Oscar Ohman had operated an ice cream store where The Park's service building is located, across from the golf course on Highland Road. When prohibition ended, Oscar got a license to sell both beer and liquor. Both operations were discontinued by 1945.

One evening back in the 1950s when we were camped at Nicolet Bay, a neighbor came over as my father was mixing up his evening cocktail. He introduced himself as Jim Tuttle from Oconomowoc. Jim had seen my father stirring his drink and asked if it was OK to consume alcohol. His inquiry was prompted because he had observed the campground was a "family" sort of place. My father assured Jim it was OK to have a drink, but then quickly added that he never mixed anything up until after five P.M.

The next day, Jim Tuttle came over shortly after four in the afternoon when my father was mixing a cocktail. Jim remarked that it wasn't five o'clock yet. My father gave him that old answer, "Well, it's five o'clock somewhere!" Our families became friends and that's how I met Robin Tuttle. Robin and I shared some dates when her parents were camped in The Park, and once, when they were not, I invited Robin to come up and camp with us when we were vacationing in The Park. I provided transportation for Robin to and from Oconomowoc.

Jim Tuttle sent some of his garden fresh green beans back with us to enjoy with our dinners. My father sent a thank-you note back to Jim a few days later when I drove Robin back home. The note was appropriately written on a piece of park stationery; a thin flat rock. Years later, my father received a small package at our home in Glen Ellyn, Illinois. Jim Tuttle had added a note on the same rock my father had sent him years earlier.

June 1, 1986

Dear Norm and Viv,

J. and J.T. (Jim and Jane Tuttle) will be "at home" at # 636 – Nicolet Bay on 7-16-86 and 7-17-86. Martinis and chicken will be served beginning at 5:00 P.M. sharp! Your attendance is requested.

I still have the rock. It brings back many memories.

Sixteen

The Huber Theater

Camping gives you time to do things you would normally not have time to do, like re-web a lawn chair, read a pile of books, write a play or be an actor in a play. Yes, I said, "Write and act in plays." There was at one time, a summer theater located at the Weborg Point campground. Mr. S. J. Huber of Portage, Wisconsin began camping at Weborg Point in 1918. Mr. Huber liked to write one act plays and found willing actors among people camped in The Park. He began staging productions in 1929.

This was a big deal! By 1934, the Huber Theater had achieved notoriety throughout Door County for producing good plays. In the early days, Huber improvised a stage at Weborg Point. But by 1934, the performances had become so popular that Superintendent Doolittle had a stage constructed, topped with a large sign made from birch branches, proclaiming it to be the Huber Theater.

The Huber Theater. Photo, Peninsula State Park

There were over 1,500 people attending the fifth annual tourist camp show held at the new theater on a Friday evening in August, 1934. The footlights of course, were gas camp lanterns. An orchestra from Sturgeon Bay provided the music. The shows were free, which might help explain the large attendance, especially since this was the height of the Depression. But a review of the performance claimed it was "highly entertaining" and there was "exceptional talent displayed."

Today, people camped at Weborg must go all the way to the Nicolet Bay Amphitheater to see a play put on by the American Folklore Theater. In the early 1930s they wouldn't have had to leave their campsite.

Seventeen

The Ski Jump

In the summer of 1935, Hjalmar Holand and Al Doolittle escorted Carl Houn through The Park searching for an area that could be used for winter sports. Mr. Houn, a civil engineer from Milwaukee, had designed major ski slides in Wisconsin. Houn recommended a location in The Park, but emphasized a county-wide organization would be required to support a winter sports operation.

In July of 1935, The Door County Sports Club was organized. Forty people attended the meeting representing communities throughout Door County. The meeting was chaired by Mr. Holand. Al Doolittle reported it might be possible to have a ski jump built by the CCC, although later in the summer, questions were raised concerning the use of CCC labor and land in a state park to support a commercial facility. But the newly formed club pressed on and in November of 1935 drew up a resolution asking the State Superintendent of Parks and Forests Harrington's support for making improvements in The Park to accommodate winter sports.

By January of 1936, Kenneth Greaves, the landscape architect working with the CCC, had made sketches of a proposed ski jump, a toboggan run and a bobsled run. These sketches were sent to Madison, Wisconsin for approval by the conservation department. Even though there was criticism of other CCC activities and plans, in the case of the winter sports project, there was good cooperation between the CCC, The Park, and local organizations. The plans Kenneth Greaves developed, were explained at a Lions Club dinner held at the CCC camp in February, 1936. At this meeting, the Lions Club expressed their thanks for the work the CCC was doing. Mr. Greaves himself was a Lion. Having laid out plans covering six months work, Mr. Greaves was transferred to Devil's Lake State Park to do planning work there.

The ski jump, toboggan run and a warming house were built. The sports area was abandoned in the early 1940s. Many cite World War

II as a cause. There was also a problem with the jump. It was located too close to the drop of the hill and considered to be unsafe. Another problem I have discovered over the years when I take my snow shoes and cross country skies to The Park on winter trips is lack of snow!

The Ski Jump. Photo, Peninsula State Park.

Around the time the winter sports area was being abandoned due to lack of use, a more significant event occurred. In 1943, Al Doolittle retired and Bill Beckstrom became the second park superintendent. Beckstrom moved up to The Park from Point Beach, and would serve as the second superintendent at Peninsula State Park until 1954.

Doolittle's vision for the winter sports area was short-lived. But most everything else he had promoted remained and was significant to The Park's early history. The roads, Eagle Tower, the trails, the golf course and especially camping in The Park, remain to remind us that Al Doolittle was the right man, at the right time, to get The Park established.

In 1964, the warming house was converted to the White Cedar Nature Center. Walk the nature trail behind the center. The toboggan run is clearly visible although trees would cause a bit of a problem if you tried to use it today. Further up the hill, you will find evidence of the steps skiers used to climb the hill. Before the old warming house became the White Cedar Nature Center, it served as a shelter building for a group camp.

Eighteen

The POW Camp

Having a German prisoner of war camp operating in the park during World War II sounds like a tremendous story. The camp was located in The Park across from the big silo on Evergreen Road, the street to your right as you enter The Park at the Fish Creek entrance. The camp operated for a brief time. German prisoners mostly did work picking cherries at local orchards.

When I think about the POW camp story, I think of a sign the owner of a stately old historic home in Janesville posted in front of his house. The sign said, "Ain't no big deal!"

In March of 1945, headlines in The Door County Advocate were proclaiming 2,000 German POW's were headed toward Door County to help with the fruit harvest. A month later, The Advocate was still saying the POW's were coming, but no one knew when. The German prisoners had been working in sugar beet fields in Nebraska or pea canneries before coming to Door County. This work delayed their arrival. The Federation of Labor protested, fearing the loss of jobs by regular orchard workers. But a shortage of labor persisted that summer because so many people, who normally would have worked in the orchards, were serving in the armed forces. By May, there were only eighty-one German Prisoners of War working at the Martins' orchard in Sturgeon Bay and people were talking of a prisoner shortage.

The orchards paid the POW's forty cents an hour. Most of the prisoner's pay was sent directly to the United States Treasury, but the prisoners got a coupon worth eighty cents for each day's work. The coupons could only be redeemed for merchandise at a POW canteen. One person became upset when seeing beer being taken out to locations where the prisoners were working. As it turned out, the beer was for the American soldiers guarding the prisoners. A friend of mine, who fought in Europe in World War II, has told me that guarding German prisoners was usually easy. Very few wanted to escape.

Victory in Europe had come on May 8, 1945 and although the war there was over, many families in Door County had lost members to the fighting in Europe. There was some understandable animosity against the POW workers. But the orchards were happy to have the help, and the POW's were happy knowing they would soon be returning to Germany. If there were any unruly prisoners, they could be segregated under guard. A silo at Martins' orchard was cited as being a good jail if needed. Perhaps the site selected in Peninsula State Park was deemed a good one because of the old silo located on Evergreen Road. The army provided tents to house the prisoners.

Eventually, nearly 2,000 POW's did assist with the 1945 cherry harvest. A small number of prisoners worked out of the Fish Creek camp in The Park for about three weeks. By mid-August, 1945, all the camps in Door County had been closed. The story about the POW camp in Peninsula State Park is no big deal, but the work done by the POW's was. The German POW's picked over a half million pails of cherries, earning over $100,000 in the process that went to the United States Treasury.

Nineteen

The First Camp

My father rode the train from Glen Ellyn, Illinois to Chicago commuting to his job. At the station each morning, he purchased a copy of the Chicago Tribune. One day in 1949, he spotted a small advertisement: Cottage with rowboat, $50 a week. That summer, we vacationed at Birchwood Cottages on Kangaroo Lake.

My father loved to fish. He spent most of the week at Kangaroo Lake in the rowboat. My mother spent most of her time cleaning fish. But we did take some car rides to explore the rest of Door County. We drove through Peninsula State Park. We saw people camping. It looked like fun. When we got home, my father consulted with a neighbor active with the Boy Scouts. That winter we ordered a tent from Sears. We did a shake down trip in June at Apple River Canyon in northwestern Illinois. In July, 1950, we were camped in The Park. I was six.

We camped at Welcker's point. The campground was located where the picnic area is today. We were the only campers there many nights.

My father made a raft for my sister and myself from logs he found along the shore. But, the logs were pretty well waterlogged, and our dreams of playing Tom Sawyer and Huck Finn taking a trip to Horseshoe Island never quite materialized.

We discovered The Park mosquitoes. Each evening at dusk, the mosquitoes came out of the woods in droves. "The mosquitoes were thick," wrote Joan Vogt in the nature center memory book many years later. I know!

We set our car top carrier on the ground behind our tent. We placed a few bags of sweet corn we had brought from our garden and other items in the open carrier. We covered it with a tarp and called it our "supply" tent. That night we were introduced to The Park raccoons. Father tried to run them off by hurling firewood at the snarling pack. He lost the battle. When we got up the next morning, we found an empty car top carrier surrounded by firewood. Of course, the sweet corn was gone. So was everything else that was edible. All that was left of a cardboard container of cocoa was the tin top and bottom. Andrew Jacobs said this about The Park raccoons writing in the nature center memory book; "They ate my mom's dental floss!" I know!

Unlike the cottage at Kangaroo Lake, our campsite did not come with a rowboat. We rented one in Ephraim and hauled it out to Welcker's Point on the roof of our car. I caught my first fish just off shore from our campsite. We were hooked on camping in The Park.

I still have a postcard my mother wrote to my grandmother. "We have a boat and have had good luck fishing. Got 15 perch (good-sized ones) and Normie got a big bass. The raccoons raid our camp every night. They ate all our sweet corn Friday night. Last night, they ate six perch." My father had left the perch we couldn't eat that night in a small live box anchored just off shore expecting to have them for breakfast. The raccoons got to them first.

Since 1950, I've camped in The Park every year except four. I missed two years beginning in 1959 when my father's job required that our family move to Switzerland. I missed another two years when I served my country as an officer in the United States Navy. But even while in the Navy, I managed to get up to The Park once. Carol Topel became my Navy bride. We were married in 1970 on a short leave I took when transferring between duty stations. We spent our honeymoon on site 636 at Nicolet Bay. Carol and I still camp in The Park every year.

Twenty

The Nicolet Bay Camp

We camped at Welcker's Point for two years. By then, my sister and I were older, and my father decided Nicolet Bay would be a better place to camp. The sand beach was a good reason to move. We pitched our tent along the shore, just north of the boat launch ramp. A small camp road provided access to this campground. A remnant of this road is the driveway leading into campsite 636. A Park ranger walked through the campground each day collecting a twenty-five cent fee. He gave us a small receipt we attached to the ridge pole of our tent to indicate we had paid. Each day, park employees dumped a huge load of firewood in a pile where the boat launch parking lot is now located. A hand pump located next to the wood pile provided water. Pit toilets were located just a hundred feet north of the water pump. No one ever got sick.

There was a large "L" shaped dock along the shore. A long arm of the dock extended out into Nicolet Bay providing protection from storms. Campers could tie their boats up at this dock and pull them up on top of the dock if a storm developed.

I spent hours fishing at this dock. My father let me use his prized J.C. Higgins bait casting reel.

A picnic and a small fish cleaning table defined a campsite. But these could be easily moved and people clustered in the more desirable areas of the campground. Those wanting privacy could stay on the fringes, but most, especially those with kids, liked to camp close to the shore where the old dock was located. Today, this area is comprised of just three camp sites, 632, 634, and 636. In the 1950s a dozen or more families pitched their tents in this area.

We met many fine people. We had to because we were camped so close together!

The Kaisers camped all summer at Nicolet Bay. They fished all day, cleaned their catch when they got back to camp and took the fish into town where they rented freezer space. They must have eaten fish all winter! One day, when it was too rough to go out in the boat, Mrs. Kaiser took a cane pole down to the dock. Before long, she had hooked a jumbo perch. Within minutes, the dock was swarming with people fishing.

We met the Krubsacks. The Krubsacks began camping in The Park in 1945. They camped at Crystal Springs campground, located along the shore at the Golf Course, straight down toward the water from the club house. This campground was closed in 1950. Dorothy Halvorsen said the campground was closed because it was difficult to patrol but also, there were complaints from people that had cottages in the area. They didn't want to look at tents. After Crystal Springs campground closed, the Krubsacks began camping at Nicolet Bay.

Ernie Krubsack owned a manufacturing company in Milwaukee and could spend quite a bit of the summer at The Park. But like other fathers who would have liked to stay with their families the entire summer, Ernie had to commute back and forth to Milwaukee on occasion to tend to his business. For a few years, the Krubsacks camped in an igloo type of structure made of lightweight fiberboard. The structure came in pieces that could be bolted together. The cold war was heating up. Ernie was making and selling these shelters to be used as temporary living quarters in case people had to evacuate a city if it suffered a nuclear attack. I don't know how many he sold for this purpose, but they did make wonderful summer camp shelters.

Sleeping and kitchen tent complete with screen door.

The Steuernagels from Milwaukee camped all summer by the old dock. They had quite a camping outfit, complete with a wooden floor that they stored during the winter with friends who lived in Fish Creek.

Below is a picture of Eve Steuernagel in their kitchen tent attached to their sleeping tent. These were some pretty fancy outfits. If you

were going to stay in The Park all summer, you wanted something comfortable.

After having spent all summer in The Park, the Steuernagels still yearned for more and often spent weekends with other friends following Labor Day at the group camp shelter which is now the nature center. Eve Steuernagel would send a letter requesting use of the shelter to The Park with a letterhead proclaiming the group to be "The Greater Milwaukee Camping Association." Eve prayed that no one at The Park office would bother to check to see if the group was actually chartered with the State of Wisconsin!

We met the Tuttles. Jim Tuttle loved to camp. His wife Jane liked things a little more on the civilized side. Every morning, Jim would get up, make a pot of coffee and coax Jane out of the tent with a steaming cup. We watched this ritual every day.

My father sitting at the "backward" fireplace.

There were fireplaces in the area built from limestone rocks held together with a little cement. One had been built with the opening facing the water. We called this the "backward" fireplace because if you sat facing the opening, your back would be facing the water. Some enterprising camper had rectified this problem by building another fireplace directly to the left of the backward one but having the opening of the new one facing the proper direction. Now while you tended your fire you could have a fine view of Nicolet Bay and Eagle Bluff.

My father's work required he travel all around the world. He had some favorite places, but none would top this spot, at this fireplace, with the view of Eagle Bluff. My father could sit for hours looking out over the old dock and Nicolet Bay as the setting sun caused the colors and light on Eagle Bluff to change in a magnificent display. It was this view that brought him back year after year to camp at this spot in The Park.

Sometimes after dinner, two young ladies would come down to the dock to play their guitars and sing folk songs until dark. These were the times my father would sit at his campfire and simply say, "I ain't mad at nobody!"

Twenty-one

The Saturday Night Campfire

I remember some wonderful entertainment at the Nicolet Bay campfires. These gatherings were held each Saturday night in the summer. The campfire program was well established when I started camping in The Park in the 1950. Its origins date back to the time when Al Doolittle was The Park superintendent.

By Saturday afternoon, park employees would have made a pile of wood eight feet in diameter and just about as high at the campfire ring close to the beach at Nicolet Bay. After dinner, campers would start to gather around the ring. The fire was lit and it became the duty of the campfire master to lead and encourage the entertainment. I remember Jeanie Copp's father as being a very accomplished campfire master.

We would sing songs, tell stories and jokes. Some people played musical instruments. People had fun! In 1992, my mother and I visited Eve Steuernagel in Milwaukee. We relived old memories by singing the "Nicolet Bay Song." This song was a Saturday night tradition and was sung to the tune of, "In a Shanty in Old Shanty Town."

It's an old canvas shanty in old Nicolet Bay,
Some round and some slanty, some every which way.
When spring rolls around, we can always be found,
Planning a trip to the old camping ground.

We'll leave all our troubles and worries behind,
We'll hidest away 'neath the moon and the pines.
We're old friends when we meet, at that perfect retreat,
Around the campfire at old Nicolet Bay.

We sang all the old favorites; Swanee River, The Old Folks at Home, I Want a Girl Just Like the Girl That Married Dear Old Dad. Then one of us kids would teach the adults the real words to "I Want a Girl."

<u>I Want a Beer</u>

I want a beer, just like the beer, that pickled dear old dad!
It was the beer and the only beer that daddy ever had.
A good old-fashioned beer, with lots of foam,
Took four men to carry daddy home!
 I want a beer, just like the beer, that pickled dear old dad!

Someone would start the echo song "You Can't Get to Heaven" and anyone with a bit of creativity could introduce the next verse.

<u>Oh You Can't Get To Heaven</u>

Leader	Oh you can't get to heaven
Group	Oh you can't get to heaven
Leader	On roller skates
Group	On roller skates
Leader	'Cause you'd roll right past
Group	'Cause you'd roll right past
Leader	Those pearly gates
Group	Those pearly gates
All	No you can't get to heaven on roller skates, 'cause you'd roll right past those pearly gates. I ain't gonna grieve my lord no more!

Next might be a rocking chair cause a rocking chair won't get you there. Or my favorite, you can't get to heaven in Mr. Copp's car; 'cause where it's going it will melt like tar!

How we would moan at the shaggy-dog stories. I remember one about five ways to get peanut butter off the roof of your mouth, none of which work except the last which would be to scrape it off with your finger which lead to another lengthy explanation of five ways to get peanut butter off your finger, none of which work except for the last of which would be to stick your finger in your mouth!

The fire would burn down. Campers would slowly retreat back to their campsites. The campgrounds would get very quiet and we all slept well.

Carol Aulabaugh standing by the faint outline of the old campfire ring.

You can still detect the outline of the fire ring at Nicolet Bay. It is just west of the swings and other playground equipment. On a quiet Saturday evening, you may still hear the singing and laughter of the campers. But now the merriment is coming from the amphitheater where everyone is being entertained by the American Folklore Theater. If Jeanie Copp's father was still here, he would be part of the American Folklore Theater cast!

Twenty-two

Doc Bush and the Dunphy

The row boats we rented in Ephraim and hauled out to camp on the roof of the car always leaked. The chances of our ever being able to afford our own boat were slim. Then my father met Doc Bush.

Doc Bush was a dentist in Appleton. Doc Bush camped in The Park, was an avid fisherman and had a Dunphy boat. Dunphy boats were made in Oshkosh, Wisconsin of molded plywood with a mahogany veneer. They were out of our price range, but we learned that Doc Bush had built his boat from a reject Dunphy hull. Doc told my father he would watch for another reject.

Doc called the day before Thanksgiving in 1954 to say a hull was available; a fourteen foot Marlin model. In the process of forming the hull, the plywood had been left in the steam bag too long and the wood turned a bit too dark and did not meet the Dunphy standard. We rented a trailer and headed to Oshkosh. We returned home with a winter project.

Every evening after dinner, Father and I retired to the garage and worked until about 10 P.M. The plywood hull contained thousands of staples that held the layers together while the hull took shape in the mold. My first lesson in boat carpentry was staple removing.

We had no building plans to follow. Every Saturday, we would drive to a boat dealer in Chicago that had a Marlin in the showroom. Father climbed all over that boat with tape measure in hand to obtain measurements for our next week's work. We bought solid brass screws by the box. Dad kept looking at the price of the screws and then glancing at the price tag on the boat in the showroom. By the time we finished the Marlin in the spring, our cost was close to the factory list price of a completed boat.

We needed a motor. The Dunphy was a sport runabout requiring a 25 HP outboard. The family savings had been depleted purchasing brass screws. A Johnson outboard was out of the question. We found a Sea King, a Johnson made for Montgomery Ward. It was last year's model and $100 less than a new Johnson. We had a motor. My uncle Gilbert gave us an old trailer originally used to transport television antenna tower sections. Using the antenna trailer as a base, we added rollers salvaged from junked wringer type washing machines and made a boat trailer.

The neighbors assembled in our driveway when we pulled the boat out for the first time. They wondered what the whining noise was coming from our garage all winter. Mostly the noise came from the DeWalt saw. Some of it came from me when I got cold. On a Sunday afternoon in 1955, we headed west to St. Charles, Illinois to launch the boat on the Fox River.

She did twenty-seven miles per hour. I was the happiest camper in The Park!

The Dunphy became an indispensable part of our camping equipment for the next 20 years. It could haul four times the amount of gear we could load in the car top carrier.

My father gave up tent camping in 1975, bought a pop-up and a small Alumacraft boat he could haul on the top of the camper. He told me he sold the Dunphy "to an old guy" and his two nephews in Door County who would use it for water skiing. I found it in 1979 parked just off Highway 42 in Ellison Bay. I poked around and could not detect any dry rot on the hull. It needed work, but it was restorable.

The next year, I didn't see the boat. A few years later I made an effort to find the owner. I was too late. I learned Gust Klenke, who owned the garage in Ellison Bay was the "old guy with the nephews" who bought the boat from my father. Gust of course was long gone. I learned one of his nephews worked as a cook at the Hillside in Ellison Bay. I stopped and enquired. Gust's nephew told me he had busted the boat up for firewood the previous winter.

I began each day in The Park by swimming out to the Dunphy to bring it in from its mooring. I would swim to the stern, unsnap the canvas cover from one corner and climb in. The smell of a mahogany hull under a canvas cover is as fresh in my mind as this morning's coffee which sits beside me now as I write this story. I still have my father's Alumacraft. It's a rowboat and it leaks.

Twenty-three

The Mooring

Keeping the boat tied up at the dock was out of the question. Even small storms produced waves that crashed over the end of the pier. A wood boat would quickly be reduced to splinters if left to bang against the dock.

The solution was to moor the boat out in the bay. We figured a garbage can full of rocks and cement would make a good anchor. Rocks were easy to find. You could buy a new garbage can at Nelsons or you could get one from the dump. We chose the dump. The dumps at Ephraim or Fish Creek were places to get many items needed in camp.

The garbage can we found had a few holes, but rocks covered most of these and once the cement set, holes would be no problem. An iron ring was imbedded in the cement at the top of the can. We rolled the garbage can from the shore onto planks straddling the gunnels of Steuernagel's boat. Very carefully, we rowed to a spot eighty feet out from where the boat ramp at Nicolet Bay is now located. Very carefully but quickly, we rolled the garbage can off the planks while simultaneously leaning out as far as we could on the opposite side of the boat. Kaploosh! The garbage can came to rest in about ten feet of water. We had a mooring!

My first job after we had camp set up each year was to put on my mask, snorkel and fins, locate the garbage can, dive down, and attach a rope. We used an old turpentine can as a buoy. Each morning, weather permitting, I would swim out to the boat, climb in, and bring it back to the dock. Oh! That water was cold! I was a skinny little kid. Pulling the starter rope of a 25 HP outboard took all the strength I could muster. That faithful Sea King always roared to life on the second pull. That was good, because I never had enough strength left for a third pull.

We used a three quarter inch hemp line on the mooring. Hemp rots. One evening, when a storm was kicking up good sized waves in Nicolet Bay, a youngster from a camp down toward the beach came running into our camp shouting, "Mr. Aulabaugh, your boat has busted loose!" Sure enough, it was heading toward the rocks on the shore. We rescued it by pushing the trailer down the shore and winching the boat up on the trailer thus keeping it from being battered to pieces. We replaced the hemp rope with a nylon line.

Twenty-four

The Dock

The dock at Nicolet Bay was the center of the universe. I got up each morning and changed into "the uniform of the day," a swimsuit. After bringing our boat in from the mooring, the days activities could begin and they all centered around this dock. The Krubsacks slid their sailboats into the water. We got out the water skis. We were ready for the day.

The dock had a diving board. The water was deep, at least eight to ten feet off the end of the board. There was a ladder so you could climb back out of the water onto the dock. The girls would lay on their beach towels to sunbathe. The boys would grab their sunglasses and throw them into the water, only to dive in and retrieve them when the girls complained. It was a good way to meet girls!

We had an old bicycle. We would tie a rope on the bike, ride it as fast as we could off the end of the long arm of the dock. We would retrieve the bicycle with the rope.

Marge Krubsack was sunbathing on the dock. Her son Roy, about two years old, was shuffling along in his older brother Kim's shoes; much too large for Roy's feet. "Mrs. Krubsack! Mrs. Krubsack! Roy just fell in!" was the cry from the kids on the dock that caused Marge to open her eyes. Marge was laying close to the edge. She rolled over, looked down into the water and there was Roy, a few feet under water, working his arms and legs as fast as he could to try and propel himself to the surface. Marge stuck her hand down, caught Roy as he broke the surface and hauled him to safety.

People were always fishing off the long arm of the dock. They would cast their lures out only to get them snagged on rocks on the bottom. Once a week, I would put on my mask and fins and snorkel around the end of the dock. I would cruise along the surface until I spotted a fish line. Even monofilament was easy to see once it had a little algae growing on it. I would dive down, grab the line and follow it to my prize. My tackle box is still full of lures I collected at the Nicolet Bay "tackle shop."

Hooks and sinkers could be collected from the logs that were underwater at the base of the dock. People would fish too close to the edge and get their hook imbedded in a log. I would cruise along these logs, about eight feet underwater collecting hooks and sinkers. Once, a large lamprey eel came slithering out from between two of the huge timbers. Snakes startle me, especially a "snake" in the water. I set a record for climbing the old dock ladder.

A young athletic couple always swam off the dock. One day, the husband organized a group of the girls that were interested in swimming to Horseshoe Island. The group dove in and swam out to the island, resting for about an hour before swimming back. The wife rowed a small boat along for safety in case anyone got tired.

Ray Steuernagel jumped into their boat from the dock. He was not wearing any shoes and landed on the edge of a coffee can full of fishing worms. Coffee cans at the time were opened with a "key" peeling off a thin strip to release the top but leaving an edge that was as sharp as a razor. Ray spent some time that day at the hospital in Sturgeon Bay getting stitches.

We tied a small piece of bacon onto a string, hung it over the edge of the dock and pulled up crabs, the tails of which, if they were "soft shells" were a favorite bait for perch.

Some idiot tied his cabin cruiser up to the dock late one Sunday with the intention of leaving it there all week while he returned to work. The boat was big and took up all the space along the side of the dock where we swam and had our diving board. When the owner came up the next weekend he found his yacht anchored out in the bay. I don't recall anyone offering him a lift out to his boat.

Late in the evening, when everything got quiet, you could walk with your girlfriend, hand in hand, out to the end of the dock and lay on your back staring up into a sky filled with billions of stars. The day always ended too soon. But it would begin again after a good night's sleep when every kid in camp would change into a swimsuit, the uniform of the day, and start it all over again.

Twenty-five
The Nicolet Bay Regatta

They were Tempest Class sailboats. The Krubsacks had two of them named after their youngest children; one was the "Roy Boy" and the other was the "Judy Lynn." They were centerboard boats with a single seventy-five square foot mainsail. Almost every day, these boats raced in the Nicolet Bay Regatta.

The racing fleet at the dock.

The Ephraim Yacht Club has a long and proud history. From the shore at Nicolet Bay, we could always see the Ephraim boats race and hear the boom of the cannon as the winner crossed the finish line. But our races at Nicolet Bay were just as exciting even though we had no cannon to signal the end of the race. Ernie Krubsack put out three floats forming a triangular race course. Each float had a red flag and was anchored to the bottom with a small weight. Round and around we went. We usually didn't even bother with a finish line. We just sailed the triangular course endlessly. If it was a race, Mr. Krubsack always seemed to win.

Ernie Krubsack found the two hulls at a lumber yard in northern Wisconsin. They were molded plywood just like our Dunphy boat. Ernie finished them off, had sails made at Joy Brothers in Milwaukee and the two perfectly matched boats became our racing fleet.

Ernie Krubsack in the Judy Lynn.

If the wind was strong, Ernie would have to sit on the side to balance the boat. If the wind was light, he sat on the bottom of the boat, leaning up against the transom with the tiller handle coming over his shoulder. He had a grin that would rival that of the Cheshire cat!

It was Ernie's skill that brought him over the finish line first. Gary, Kim and I could switch boats with him and he would still win. Gary and Kim sometimes threatened to tie tin cans on their father's centerboard to slow him down.

Few people know it, but Nicolet Bay once had a fog horn. Ernie was out sailing around Horseshoe Island. A fog bank rolled in. We got worried. Ernie never carried a compass. Marge drove their car down to the dock. Every thirty seconds she gave a blast on the horn. She did this for over an hour. Finally, Ernie slowly appeared out of the fog. Showing his usual big grin he hollered to Marge on the dock, "Thanks for firing up the fog horn!" His grin was only surpassed by the look of relief on Marge's face.

Gary liked to pull the sheet line in tight in a stiff breeze until the boat had a gunwale almost in the water. Then he would tip it a little more and holler "shipping water" as water flowed in over the gunwale. This was a fairly safe maneuver as long as Gary let the sheet line out before the boat took on too much water. But if Gary was not quick enough, over she would go. We lost a nice nylon line that way and Mr. Krubsack was not too happy.

In 1986, I saw what must surely be a Krubsack boat sailing on the bay. Impossible I thought, because I knew these boats had not been on Nicolet Bay for at least twenty years. Later in the day, the boat was gone. I figured it must belong to someone camping in the area. I rode my bicycle up and down the camp roads until I spotted the boat on a small trailer. A young lady at the campsite was tending her fire. I stopped and said, "You must know Ernie Krubsack." Without hesitating she said, "Yes, he's my uncle." I met Erica. It came as no surprise to her that I had identified that she was related to Ernie Krubsack because of the boat. They were unique. I once looked up the tempest class to see if they were still being made. There is such a class today, but the boats are nothing like the two Ernie had. Erica called it her little sailing bathtub and said she would never part with it.

I visited Marge and Ernie Krubsack in 1991 at their home at Hot Springs, Arkansas. I was there to gather information for this book. I learned that Erica had died a year earlier from a brain tumor. I'm still searching for one of those sailing bathtubs.

Twenty-six

Putting the Ladies Down

Walt Richter, his wife Helen and their twin boys camped in The Park each summer. Walt was an engineer for an electric utility in Milwaukee, but he had a more interesting occupation on the side. He was a diver. Not a scuba diver, but a diver that went below using air delivered through a hose attached to his diving gear. Walt used this gear to keep the water intakes for the city of Milwaukee clear of debris. He also salvaged all kinds of things that fell into the lake including one airplane. He had a small barge he used in his salvage operation and also used this equipment to take in and put out the buoys at the South Shore Yacht Club in Milwaukee each year. But most of all, Walt had a real passion. He liked "putting the ladies down."

Walt Richter, second from left, fitting the face mask on Evelyn Marsh.
The gas engine with air pump is on the dock between Walt and Evelyn.

When Walt came up to The Park, he brought along a diving rig consisting of a small Briggs and Stratton engine that ran an air pump, a long length of air hose, a face mask to wear underwater that allowed you to breathe air from the hose, and some weights to keep you on the bottom. Walt would let just about anyone dive with his gear, but he really liked letting the ladies give it a try.

My father was always telling people about how wonderful it was to camp in The Park. Ed Gartz, a good friend of my father's, decided to give it a try. The Gartzs had two young children and the family took to camping from the first day. One day Mrs. Gartz took the two children down to the dock to swim. They were gone a long time. Ed went down to see how things were going. When he got to the dock, there was a small crowd of people standing around a gas engine running an air pump. His two children were there but he did not see his wife. He inquired as to where she was. Walt Richter pointed to the hose that led from the pump into the water. About thirty feet out from the dock you could clearly see bubbles rising to the surface.

Ed was not a happy camper! I can still hear Ed scolding his wife when she finally surfaced and climbed back on the dock. "You could have killed yourself – what about the kids – don't you think about the kids – they don't want to grow up without a mother!"   But Mrs. Gartz didn't hear a thing he was saying; she was still so excited about her dive. And Walt Richter had done once again what he did so well, "putting the ladies down."

Twenty-seven

The Nicolet Bay Water-Ski School

The day we first launched the Dunphy, my father saw an "old guy" water-skiing. Dad decided that if that "old guy" could water-ski, so could he. He bought a pair of skis.

My father taught himself how to water-ski. He had watched others and just followed their lead. My father hollered "hit it" and I crammed the throttle lever full forward on the Dunphy.   Father rose out of the water and remained on the skis with his third try. He almost made one full lap around Nicolet Bay before he tumbled. But he was hooked and he taught countless others how to ski. My sister, Sandy and I were next. Father would stay in that cold water patiently holding the tips of our skis up as we made attempt after attempt to "get up" on the skis. We finally mastered the process. Then he taught others. Gary and Kim Krubsack were next, then their father Ernie Krubsack, then the other kids that were always hanging around the dock. Everyone graduated from my father's Nicolet Bay Water-Ski School. Everyone, that is, except my mother.

My mother had no sense of balance. I had tried to teach her how to ride a bicycle with disastrous results. The minute I let go of the bicycle – CRASH! It was no different with water-skis. At first, Mother forgot to let go of the rope if her attempt failed. She bounced all over the bottom of Nicolet Bay hanging onto that tow rope. Mom insisted she swallowed so much water trying to learn to ski, that the bay dropped a foot. She was a good sport and kept trying, but after a few years, we gave up. Mother was never going to water-ski.

I hollered "hit it" and popped out of the water. Easy to do when you are 10.

We skied after breakfast until lunch. After lunch, we skied until dinner. I would make two trips a day over to Ephraim in the boat to buy gas at Eagle Inn Dock. Gas with oil premixed in it sold for fifty cents a gallon and quickly became our major camping expense. I often saw Mother counting the money she had set aside in her purse for our vacation, wondering if we were going to eat or ski. Fortunately she hid a few dollars so we could buy gas to get home.

I built a saucer from a half sheet of plywood. It was simply a round disk, but what fun we had with it. I took a lawn chair with me on the disk and rode in style sitting on the chair until I wasn't careful and allowed the forward edge of the saucer to dig into the water. The saucer would head for the bottom. I could see it descend into the depths and finally begin to rise back to the surface. It would waffle back and forth as it came up gaining speed as it came. I got whacked badly just once. After that, I would try to determine where it would surface and swim like crazy away from that place!

Ernie Krubsack was a tough customer; a big powerful man. He was a good skier and loved to jump the boat wake. He would swing far out to one side of the Dunphy, then cut back digging the skis in so he moved almost perpendicular to the travel of the boat, gaining speed as he went, and then leaping over the wake. When he did this, he pulled so hard on the tow rope that the Dunphy almost slowed to a stop, the outboard churning the water, but the boat going nowhere. Of course, Ernie was going somewhere at lightening speed! By the time he was through with the maneuver, he sank at least up to his knees as the boat struggled to gain speed once again. But I never saw Ernie fall.

Falling was bad news because the water was so cold. I learned to launch from the dock so I didn't have to get wet. I would sit on the edge of the dock, water-skis dangling out over the water, about 20 feet of slack in the tow rope and yell "hit it!" The Dunphy would accelerate, take the slack out of the rope and yank me off the dock. If I leaned back just enough, I could remain upright when the skis hit the water. Coming back in was more difficult. The trick was to drop the tow rope at the right moment, glide up to the dock and catch the diving board. If I let go of the rope too soon, I sank helplessly a few feet from the diving board. If I held on too long and came in too fast, I had to purposefully dive into the water to avoid hitting the dock. But if I was successful with the launch and landing, I didn't have to get wet!

Carl Fiala and his friend Bobby Vlach had a boat and were good skiers. Carl was good at launching from the dock. Unfortunately, Carl had been camping for most of the summer, wearing the same swimsuit. The swimsuit suffered badly from dry rot. Bobby yanked Carl off the dock. It was a good take off, except Carl's swimsuit was left hanging on the head of a nail that snagged it as Carl launched. Carl had a great tan and he looked like the old Coppertone ad on skis. We all stood on the dock pointing. Carl quickly realized what had happened, let go of the rope and dove into the bay. He climbed into the boat on the side away from the dock, and disappeared across the bay to where he and Bobby were camped. Carl returned a few minutes later skiing in a pair of blue jeans!

One ski over the shoulder, the other on the water.
And with Eagle Bluff in the background
it just does not get any better.

We made a pair of "shoe skis" so we could do tricks. As always, when we needed to make something, we went shopping at the dump. We found an old pair of rubber boots, nailed these to two short pieces of wood and viola, shoe skis. If you were careful, you could turn around and ski backwards and do other tricks.

My dad made the cover of The Resorter Reporter insert to the Door County Advocate. It wasn't a complimentary photo. Father had launched from the dock, leaned back a bit too far and was dragging his butt in the water, creating quite a wake as he struggled to stand straight up on the skis. Someone at his office got a copy of the paper. When my father retired, his co-workers gave him a framed copy of the Reporter along with a slalom ski. The ski had a post mounted on the front supporting a cup holder for his coffee and a bicycle horn to warn people to get out of his way. When my father sold the Dunphy to Gust Klenke, his Nicolet Bay Water-Ski School closed its doors forever.

Twenty-eight

The Fireplace

I was tempted to write, "On the following page is a list of all the wonderful recipes you can prepare on a Wisconsin DNR fire ring." Then I was going to purposefully leave the following page blank. I've changed my mind for three reasons. First, a blank page in the middle of a book leads some people to return the book thinking it is defective. Second, a Peninsula Park camp cook book, created with the assistance of the Peninsula Golf Association, Sara Blackwood, Kathleen Harris and others, contains many good recipes for things you can actually prepare on a DNR fire ring. And third, I bought one of those tripod grills that will straddle a DNR fire ring and allows me to control the heat by raising and lowering the height of the grill over the fire. I've finally discovered how to cook on a DNR fire ring.

However, I still insist that nothing will equal the cooking ability of a camp fireplace made of Door County limestone. We always built our own fireplace. My father was so particular about the stones he used; he would drive over to Tennison Bay to get the best. A good fireplace required a base layer made of rocks, each one at least fifteen inches long, eight inches wide and six inches thick. Succeeding layers could contain rocks not quite as thick as the base layer. As the fire would burn down, layers could be removed thus lowering the grill.

My father cooked over cedar coals. He would start his fire at least two hours before he began cooking, allowing the cedar to burn just enough to form a bed of thick coals.

My father was known for his camp chicken. One of our neighbors, Ed Dorsey, would fly up to The Park on weekends just to eat that chicken. My father would cook a cut up chicken over his cedar coals for two hours. After the fat had dripped out from the skin, he would begin basting each piece with melted butter seasoned with garlic, salt and pepper. When the fire had completely burned down, Father claimed he could keep the chicken going for another two hours on the heat the limestone rocks had absorbed!

My father worked magic with that fireplace. He could shrink a bratwurst down to the size of a pork sausage. He cooked extra thick pork chops with a perfection I have never experienced elsewhere. Mother always bought our meat from Dorothy Alwes, who ran a grocery store and meat market in Fish Creek, where the On Deck store is located now. We wrapped potatoes in aluminum foil, placed them directly on the coals and ate them topped with cream style corn. Ed Dorsey introduced us to onions baked in the campfire. We cooked them just like the potatoes. If you let them caramelize on the outside they are wonderful. If you leave them in the fire too long and they burn a little, they are still wonderful.

Building our camp fireplace was a tradition for years. But it was hard on the environment. People would build them too close to trees creating a fire hazard and scorching overhead limbs. Heat destroys natural nutrients and bacteria in the soil. Fireplaces built in constantly moving locations were not good for the campsites. So DNR fire rings were installed.

But the tradition of building your own fireplace lived on and didn't die easily. Everyone got the message one year when we found a sign at the entrance to the north Nicolet Bay camp area.

Carol said, "Look – they put up a sign just for you!" I was one of the guilty ones. I've found that with the tripod, I can make chicken almost as good as my father used to cook on his limestone rock fireplace. But there are still some things you can't cook on a DNR fire ring. Jessica Brookie wrote the following in a memory book entry at the nature center, "Jiffy Pop doesn't work on a campfire." I assume Jessica was referring to the microwave version. On a later page, Andrew Minton, age 10 said, "The meal I like to make is shicka bobs!"

Now would be a good time to mention something about the scientific experiments involving fireplaces that have been conducted in The Park for years. These experiments are repeated over and over with the same results. We do not need to conduct them anymore. Glass bottles and tin cans, do not burn! Please, enough experiments!

Now would also be a good time to say something about firewood. Don't bring firewood from home to The Park. This practice is spreading pests and diseases that threaten trees in The Park. The emerald ash borer is one such serious threat. Buy your wood in The Park or from some other local source that obtains their wood from the immediate area.

And finally, this story would not be complete without mentioning the "ceremony of the hollow log." Elmer and Clara Logemann were friends of the Steuernagels. Like others, they camped all summer at Nicolet Bay. Elmer introduced us to hollow logs. Elmer was pretty particular about his logs. He would drive up to Gills Rock to one particular wood yard which had, in his opinion, the best hollow logs in

Door County. After your campfire burns down, you place your hollow log vertically over the coals. Sometimes, I place the log on two small pieces of firewood laid parallel over the coals so a little air can get in under the log. After a while, the log blazes with a spectacular effect.

Note my father's limestone rock fireplace. However, DNR fire rings work just as well with hollow logs. You don't need to drive to Gills Rock to get a hollow log. Just ask the Olsons who run the wood yard in The Park for one. They usually have a few set aside. The Olsons call them "chimney logs." You need to remind them they are properly called hollow logs. Tell them to ask Elmer Logemann. He knows.

Twenty-nine

The Endless Summer

By 1956, we knew the Steuernagels, the Krubsacks, and other families that camped all summer at Nicolet Bay very well. The fathers of these families would set up camp in June after the children got out of school, camp with the family for the duration of their vacation and then become weekend commuters for the rest of the summer.

When my father's two-week vacation was over in 1956, he asked my mother if she wanted to stay another week with "the kids." Mother said, "Yes." My sister and I were somewhat more vocal. Yes! Yes! Yes! We had the boat so we could get to Ephraim or Fish Creek for ice and groceries and other campers with cars were also happy to give us a lift into town.

Our endless summer camp.

My dad came back the next Friday night. When Sunday came, he again asked my mother if she wanted to stay another week with "the kids." Again she said, "Yes!" This went on for the rest of the summer.

Every Friday night, Mother would fix dinner for me and my sister at the usual time and then about 9 P.M. she would get a campfire going so my father could cook a steak when he arrived shortly after ten. On Sunday night, my father would set his alarm before he climbed into his sleeping bag, get up a little before 4 A.M. on Monday morning, heat some water on the Coleman stove to shave and head back to his "other" job in Chicago.

There were no flush toilets, no showers. We kids didn't worry about taking a bath. We went swimming every day, and that was enough to keep us clean. I bragged I had not touched a bar of soap all summer! But, for my father, who had to go back to work each Monday not smelling like a campfire, bathing was a necessity!

One Friday night, it began to rain shortly after my mother got the campfire going for my father's steak. My sister and I were already tucked away in our sleeping bags in the tent. Mom kept piling wood on the fire and kept it going until Dad arrived. While my father cooked his steak, my mother held a tin plate over it so the salt, pepper and garlic would not be washed away by the pouring rain. When the steak was done, they hurried to our tent to get out of the rain. The Steuernagels had observed the whole process, and hollered out insisting they come over to their kitchen tent to eat. My mother and father gladly accepted their invitation. That night, my parents were introduced to cherry bounce. The recipe is simple. Take a quart canning jar, fill it with Door County cherries and then pour in bourbon until the jar was full. Cap it up; set it on a shelf for a year, and viola – cherry bounce! You can substitute gin or vodka for the bourbon if you choose.

How can you keep yourself busy throughout an endless summer? It was easy. We rode our bicycles everywhere. Ray Steuernagel's bicycle went down the old ski hill one day, fortunately without a rider. Gary Krubsack and I rode our bicycles on Eagle Trail once. Well, actually, we pushed them over rocks most of the way. Back then, Eagle Trail ascended a long flight of stairs to Eagle Terrace. We carried our bicycles up the stairs. Please note, bicycles are no longer allowed on hiking trails.

We rode our bicycles on all The Park roads and past the small group of trees in the little "island" on Skyline Road. A sign identified the group of trees as "The Apostles." I stopped once to count the trees. There were only eleven. I pondered this problem for some time until my sister asked me if I really considered Judas an apostle. The number of trees representing the apostles has dwindled to ten. The sign is gone.

After dark, some of the older kids would go to Blossomburg Cemetery and tell ghost stories. I was too young and Mother would not let me go, but my older sister would gladly relate the tales to me when she returned hoping to ruin my sleep that night.

We picked buckets of choke cherries once, proudly presenting them to my mother and imploring her to make jelly. Poor Mother bought sacks of sugar trying to sweeten the juice enough to make it edible. Mom tried, but the jelly never jelled. We finally used the juice on pancakes as syrup.

The navigation aid on the south side of Horseshoe Island used to be powered with Edison batteries. They looked a lot like a regular automobile battery but were not rechargeable. The coast guard was not very ecologically minded at the time. The old batteries were tossed into a pile behind the light at the end of their service life. We would scrounge through the pile, looking for a recently discarded battery that did not have a cracked case. Such batteries usually had some life left in them. We hauled them back to camp, wired up a flashlight bulb and had a dandy night light.

The Krubsacks had a rowboat with a viewing port in the bottom. The port was a round piece of glass about three inches in diameter. One person at a time could lie in the bottom of the boat exploring the depths while another rowed. Gary, Kim and I spent hours peering through this glass.

One evening, an "ocean liner" sailed through Nicolet Bay. We had just finished washing the dishes. I looked up and saw it." No fooling, this thing was HUGE! Gary Krubsack and I raced to launch his rowboat to investigate. The "ocean liner" was actually the Chanticleer from New York. The Chanticleer, a 110 foot long Burger motor yacht, was owned by Ralph Evinrude, the son of Ole Evinrude. Ole Evinrude developed his outboard motor in 1909 having once rowed a small boat on a very hot day to get ice cream for Bessie Emily Cary, the girl he would eventually marry. "Why row when you can use a light weight detachable motor," Ole would say!

Ralph Evinrude and his wife, the singer and actress Francis Langford, spent a lot of time sailing the Great Lakes in the Chanticleer. Gary and I didn't see Ralph Evinrude or Francis Langford that evening. But racks displaying the entire line of Evinrude outboard motors on each side of the yacht left no doubt as to who owned the boat. The Chanticleer headed off in the direction of Ephraim. Gary and I couldn't pursue it very far. We were rowing.

We stayed that summer until Labor Day. My mother remembers two problems as a result of our endless summer. Once we got home, she couldn't get out of the habit of brushing crumbs off the table onto the kitchen floor. She also had to constantly remind my sister and me to flush!

Nothing I have ever done has left me with as many fond memories, as that endless summer I spent camping in The Park.

Thirty
The Three Week Rule

Nothing in the history of The Park, affected campers more than "the three week rule." The rule could be stated simply, but it impacted camping greatly. The rule required campers leave The Park for one week after they had camped in The Park for three weeks. The three week rule ended the endless summers. The families that camped all summer with fathers commuting to The Park on weekends were no longer able to do so because of the new rule. Without "permanent" campers, the Saturday night campfires became a thing of the past. It was the popularity of camping in The Park that required the establishment of the rule. The Park was getting too crowded. The campers that stayed all summer took the choice campsites and held them from Memorial Day to Labor Day. The three week rule was necessary. But at the same time, the rule brought a wonderful camping tradition in The Park to a close.

Some of the people, who previously camped in The Park all summer, moved to other Wisconsin parks where there was still no time limit. Ernie Krubsack had a better idea. He bought two acres of land from Carl Anderson on Middle Road.

Carl Anderson was born in Sweden in 1885. He came to the United States in 1914. Carl was living in Chicago when he was diagnosed with tuberculosis. Carl's doctor did not hold out much hope for him, but said moving to a place where the air was better than in Chicago might help. Carl Anderson moved to Door County. He lived to be 91 years old.

In 1926 Carl purchased 40 acres from Augusta and Alfred Olson who still owned land on Middle Road in The Park. About 300 acres of land in The Park was not acquired when The Park was created in 1909. The 40 acres Carl purchased was part of this land still not owned by The Park. Carl built a greenhouse on his property and lived there until the mid-1960s.

In August of 1957, Ernie Krubsack, not wanting to give up his summers in The Park because of the three week rule, bought two acres of land from Carl Anderson for $1,000. Ernie moved his trailer up to his newly acquired acres from his campsite on Nicolet Bay and continued to enjoy endless summers in The Park. This is how I came to know Carl Anderson.

Carl Anderson made a modest living selling flowers he raised in his greenhouse in the summer and Christmas trees he raised on his land and sold in the winter for fifty cents each. Carl was a bachelor and lived very simply. He did not have a car. He walked into town or got a ride with friends. He had a small Delco power plant that supplied electricity to run a pump so he could get water. Gary Krubsack and I loved to visit Carl and ask him to start his power plant, which he always did. But he shut it down after just a few seconds. He didn't want to use up his gasoline. Carl was well-educated and very interested in politics.

Every morning, the Krubsacks would ride their bicycles down to Nicolet Bay. Ernie would bring the gear they needed for the day in the family station wagon. Getting down to the bay was easy because it was downhill most of the way. At the end of the day, Ernie would tow everyone back up to their place on Middle Road. Ernie had small ropes hanging out the back of his station wagon. Everyone would take a rope, bring it around the steering post on their bicycle, put the end under their hand on the handlebar, and off the caravan would go.

Seven other families purchased parcels ranging from one to two acres from Carl. A plat map from the time shows a private road, twenty feet wide, leading into eight pieces of property subdivided from Carl Anderson's forty acres on Middle Road.

This arrangement did not last for long. On February 8, 1960, the State of Wisconsin started condemnation proceedings against all the land owners including Carl. Some of the people tried to fight the process. Marge and Ernie quietly gave in to the state. They realized the land really belonged to The Park. They had simply purchased a few more "endless summers" in The Park. Now it had to come to an end.

Years earlier, The Park had tried to buy Carl's 40 acres for $2,500 or about $62 an acre. When the state purchased Carl's land as a result of the 1960 proceedings, they had to pay $500 an acre, the price established by what the Krubsacks had paid. Ernie had a twinkle in his eye and that Cheshire cat grin when he told me this story. Ernie Krubsack lost his land in The Park, but as a result, he had helped Carl Anderson get a higher price for his!

Carl was allowed to remain living at his green house even after The Park had acquired his property. But finally, poor health forced Carl Anderson to move to the Dorchester Nursing Home in Sturgeon Bay. Whenever Ernie Krubsack visited Carl at Dorchester, he always brought him a small bottle of brandy, something perhaps forbidden, but favorably received by the old bachelor from Sweden.

Thirty-one

Trouble in The Park

There was trouble in Lake Geneva, Wisconsin over the Fourth of July holiday in 1966. It began when thousands of young people created a disturbance that got out of control and evolved into a full-fledged riot. A year later, there were problems again at Lake Geneva, but the authorities were better prepared and kept a lid on the trouble. With the lid placed on the situation at Lake Geneva, some of the troublemakers headed north to Door County.

Door County Sheriff Bridenhagen estimated there were about 1,500 young people in Door County over the July 4, 1967 holiday that had spilled over from Lake Geneva. In Door County, the worst trouble was at the Parkway Bar, a "beer" bar which served beer only, to persons 18 years of age or older. The Old Parkway Bar is now the English Inn on Highway 42 between Fish Creek and Ephraim. The owner of The Parkway requested police assistance to close his place down on Saturday night when the youth started getting extremely rowdy. People were still talking about the problems at the Parkway when I arrived at The Park to camp in August.

But the trouble spilled over into The Park as well. The police confiscated many cases of beer from under aged youth in The Park. There were over 100 arrests that weekend and half of them were made in Peninsula State Park. Some of the people causing trouble were getting high on marijuana and hallucinogenic drugs. Sheriff Bridenhagen reported there were 10 hippies sitting in a pine tree in The Park, "hooting like owls and howling like Coyotes!" Fortunately, the weather turned cold and rainy and helped keep a lid on things.

Lynn Hanson, The Park manager, got called to duty to take care of a lady, high on marijuana, who had gone into the water at Nicolet Bay and decided she didn't need a swim suit anymore. Lynn remembered having to get a rope around the unruly naked lady to haul her out of the water. Lynn got a lot of kidding about having to "rescue" a naked lady. Yes, it was a tough job, but somebody had to do it!

No one likes to see any trouble in The Park. This is a family place. Park Superintendent Tom Blackwood welcomes visitors to The Park to enjoy the top Midwest camping spot as determined by Midwest Living Magazine and the best place to picnic according to Wisconsin Trails magazine. Tom also encourages visitors to enjoy hiking, biking, nature study, golfing, swimming, and all the other fine activities The Park provides. Getting intoxicated, reckless driving and causing trouble anywhere in the park is not on anyone's list of things to do in The Park. The Park staff and volunteer camp hosts do a good job to ensure that The Park provides a positive experience for all visitors. But for one Fourth of July, there was trouble in The Park!

Thirty-two

Courting the Ladies

The Park was, and still is, a good place for courting the ladies. A happy couple can take long walks, spend romantic times around a campfire, gaze up at millions of stars on a dark night and if they are real lucky, catch the moon rising. It starts as a big orange ball rising up over Ephraim and later, higher in the sky, sends its shimmering silver reflection over the waters of Nicolet Bay. It just does not get any better than this.

It was on just such an evening that my mother and father decided to drive up to Sven's Bluff to watch the lights of Marinette and Menomince across Green Bay. They had been "parked" there for a while, when there was a light rapping on the window. It was pretty late. Of course, the rapping on the window was being done by a park ranger. My father rolled his window down. The ranger saw my father's very bald head and just said, "Excuse me, sir!"

There were always many things to do in addition to romantic activities in The Park. The movie at the Sky View changed every third night. There were plays at The Peninsula Players. A soda at Wilson's was always a treat. But many of the potential dates I met were working summer jobs in the area and did not want to become involved with someone who was going to be there for only a week or two. I solved the problem by "importing" my dates.

I had a small pup tent I had used as a boy scout. This kept things respectable. I could sleep in the main tent with my parents and the girlfriends could stay in the pup tent. The arrangement worked well.

I met Carol Topel at Northern Illinois University in the fall of 1967. I invited Carol to camp the next year. Carol had never camped before. The first night, raccoons snarling outside her tent kept her up most of the night. But she was a good sport and soon settled into the camping routine. We celebrated her birthday by putting candles in a cherry pie. My folks gave her a birthday card which was a note written on a piece of flat rock. And, because of Carol, I got to know Dr. Sneeberger in Ephraim.

We were returning to camp late one evening after seeing a movie at the Sky View. It must have been something Carol ate. She started to have a severe allergic reaction, broke out in hives, and was having serious problems breathing. We were just coming into the Park. I asked the person on duty at The Park office where I could find a doctor. The answer was Dr. Sneeberger. His house was located next to Wilson's in Ephraim. There was still a light on upstairs at the Sneeberger residence. I knocked on the door. A lady let us in.

Dr. Sneeberger recognized the allergy problem immediately. A huge dose of benadryl was needed. The good doctor was very old. I watched as he filled a syringe, his hands shaking with a noticeable tremor. But they became rock steady just as he started to give the injection. Within an hour, Carol was breathing easy. I was charged $20.

Before locating in Door County, Dr. Sneeberger practiced in the small town of Orfordville, Wisconsin where Carol and I now live. Not many people in Orfordville still remember Dr. Sneeberger, but Carol and I do! Dr. Sneeberger is buried in Blossomburg Cemetery and Carol and I pay our respects each time we visit The Park.

In 1969, Uncle Sam made me a job offer I couldn't refuse. I could either be drafted into the Army for two years or enlist in the Navy for four. I chose the Navy. After boot camp, I was stationed at Pensacola, Florida. My pay was $135 a month. Then I received orders to officer candidate school. My pay increased substantially which made marriage an economic possibility. When Carol said yes, marriage really became a possibility! We were married on June 6, 1970. Carol's mother was her matron of honor. My father was my best man. What a best man! He packed the Dunphy with camping gear and let us use his car to pull the boat up to The Park for our honeymoon.

We honeymooned on campsite 636. In 1980, we saw a young couple getting married at the amphitheater. Last year I read a nature center memory book entry about a couple that got married at Eagle Terrace. Why didn't I think of something creative like this! Carol and I limited our wedding guests to our immediate families. We could have fit everyone on top of Eagle Tower! We plan to renew our vows on June 6, 2020, our fiftieth wedding anniversary, at the tower, if it's still there and we're able to climb the stairs!

Carol slaving over a hot camp stove on our honeymoon.

Thirty-three

Getting There is Half the Fun

The 1921 visitors guide had a section titled, "How to get there." The prospective visitor was told they could reach The Park by auto stage from Sturgeon Bay, or by taking one of the Goodrich boats from Milwaukee. I made my first trip in a 1950 Plymouth. We left before sunrise. Mother filled the green Stanley thermos with coffee. My father stopped after a few hours at a wayside to have a sweet roll and coffee. My sister and I slept in the back seat. Getting there is still half the fun.

When I got out of the Navy we settled in Janesville, Wisconsin. Carol and I constructed a camp kitchen box made of plywood we painted green. We affectionately call it "the green box." It holds all the kitchen "stuff" we need at camp. Leaving everything in the green box assures we won't forget the essential kitchen items like the ice pick, extra mantles for the lantern, a cork screw and the all important camp coffee pot. When we haul the green box up from the basement, the anticipation starts to build. It's a good feeling, a happy feeling, and a testament to how important The Park is in our lives.

In the 1970s and early 1980s when we could still get a campsite on a first come first served basis, we would head out to The Park on Friday night right after work. Sometimes we stopped at Smith Brothers in Port Washington for dinner. If we didn't eat at Smith Brothers we could stop anywhere because it was Friday night in Wisconsin and every supper club, restaurant or bar along the way served a great fish fry. After dinner, we would drive on further and finally stop at a motel. We have stayed at every motel between Milwaukee and Algoma at least once!

One year, we stopped just outside Belgium, north of Port Washington. We drove into town to find a place for dinner. A heavy fog was being swept inland from the lake. We stopped to watch the local softball game. Because of the fog, the lights at the ballpark had come on early. It was a surrealistic scene. The bleachers were filled with every age group. The fog kept whirling through this scene, isolating the ball game from the rest of the world. Everything that is right about small town America was there that evening.

The drive up Wisconsin's "East Coast" is magic. So many memories. In 1950, I heard Ernie Von Schledhorn on a Milwaukee radio station ask his famous question, "Who do you know wants 'ta buy a car?" Today I see the statement on a billboard when passing the dealership. We exit the interstate to drive through downtown Port Washington. Seeing St. Mary's church on the hill reassures me that some things never change.

As we got close to Manitowoc, we would tune in the Chilton, Wisconsin radio station that played polkas twenty-four hours a day. It no longer does. Today we slip a tape with polka music into the tape deck instead. At Manitowoc we exit the interstate and drive straight to the lake on Waldo Boulevard. When I was a kid, my father always told us the road went into the lake and we believed him! At least it looked like it did as we traveled east on the boulevard. I always tell Carol this story. Even though she had heard it dozens of times, she never complains.

A little further on at Rostok, we pass Van's Supper Club that used to entice you to stop for a meal with their sign "Slam on your brakes for Butch Van's steaks!" The sign is gone; the old supper club is now surrounded with a chain link fence and a large sign on the roof says "Fireworks."

At Algoma, we turn onto County S and follow the shore. I tune the radio to WDOR when the small sign along the road tells us we have just passed from Kewaunee to Door County.

I'm superstitious. I always cross over the old downtown bridge in Sturgeon Bay on my way north and use the new Highway 42 bridge when traveling south. I was certain a great tragedy would occur the year the downtown bridge was closed for repairs and I had to use the new bridge on our way heading north.

Outside Sturgeon Bay, where Highway 57 splits from Highway 42, there used to be a sign proclaiming, "There's more to do on 42!" I always tell Carol the story as we pass this spot.

At the bottom of the hill in Egg Harbor, I check to see if the tepee is still out front of the Chief Oshkosh trading post. Just north of Egg Harbor, is the house where a small sign indicated this was the home of the world famous Follets Watch Us Grow Company. At Juddville, we pass Mr. Robertoy's place where he tended his raspberries and sold firewood. A very small sign close to the road simply said, "firewood." Mr. Robertoy and his raspberries are gone. We buy our firewood today from the Olsons at The Park wood yard. We descend the hill into Fish Creek and drive past the old stores that used to be run by Dorothy Alwes and Ed Schreiber. We're almost there and getting there is half the fun because it brings back so many memories.

Thirty-four

The Last Days of the Dock

The dock was a magnificent structure. It survived summer storms and winter ice for years. I swam from this dock. I water-skied from this dock. I tied the Dunphy up at this dock. We sailed from this dock. And one day, I caught the dock in a rare state – there were no people or boats on the dock. There was only an inner tube hanging on the corner by the swim ladder and one stone on the extension to the right where the Krubsacks used to pull their sailboats out of the water.

No one on was on the diving board next to the swim ladder. The boards were weathered to an unforgettable grey color. This is how I want to remember the dock. I only have memories now, because the dock is gone.

It was 1974. The Park had tried to save the dock. A few years earlier, the thick wood planks on the top had been removed and cement poured to form a new surface. But the water levels were rising each year to unprecedented heights. The water, at least four feet higher than the level shown in the previous picture, came right up over the top of the dock. This allowed the winter ice to slide over the dock, crushing it. The dock began to break up. By the end of the summer in 1974, it was almost gone.

Kids were still swimming off the dock. My father still pulled his Alumacraft up on the dock. People still sunbathed on the dock. But the dock was dying.

I walk the shoreline today looking for evidence of the old dock. It's hard to find any. The water used to be over ten feet deep right along this shore. The dock held the shoreline back from the deep area dredged out of the bay. The shoreline has reclaimed the depths. I snorkel along the shore and can still find a few traces of the old logs. But the dock is gone.

Entropy – the process, where things that have been built by man or by nature, eventually degrade back to their original state.

Thirty-five

The Other Docks

There were a number of old docks and piers located in The Park. There is a concrete dock along the shore at the lighthouse. When the water was low, it sat high and dry on the shore as it does today. When the water was high, I once drifted the Alumacraft right over the top. The only dock in The Park that still survives is located at Weborg Point, although it hardly resembles the original because it has been enlarged and reconstructed so many times over the years.

You can still find underwater remnants of a magnificent old dock along the shore by the golf course. Start at the opening in the trees where the golf course comes down almost to the water's edge. Stay just out from the edge of the drop off and head north toward the end of Eagle Bluff. The water must be calm so you can see into the depths. You will soon pass over some huge ancient cribs that were part of a wood dock operated by Sorn Hanson in the 1800s. Docks were built by constructing cribs built on the winter ice. The cribs were huge square structures made of logs and filled with rock. When the ice melted in the spring, the cribs would sink to the bottom providing platforms for constructing the dock. If the water is calm, you can clearly see the ancient cribs that formed the Hanson dock. This is a good place to fish. But I just like to float silently over these old cribs, marvel at their size and think about the stories they could tell.

There are some small cribs in the bay at Weborg Point. These cribs probably supported a footbridge that connected the point with land to the south eliminating the necessity for the early settlers in the area from having to travel all the way around the sedge meadow to get into Fish Creek. These cribs can easily be accessed with a snorkel and fins.

Entropy – the process, where things that have been built by man or by nature, eventually degrade back to their original state.

Thirty-six

The Bird Man

We knew of Paul Blanchard long before we knew Paul Blanchard. Carol and I first saw him peddling a bicycle around Nicolet Bay. The bicycle had a child carrier mounted behind the seat, but instead of a child, the carrier was loaded with camera equipment. Paul would stop and set up his camera along with an elaborate system of mirrors. He used the mirrors to reflect additional light on a bird nest he wanted to photograph. Every year, we would see Paul somewhere in The Park, always photographing birds. We called him, "the bird man" until Mary Ellen Connor introduced us one spring day. Mary Ellen and Don Connor from Rockford, Illinois camped each summer at Nicolet Bay.

Paul was a professor of mathematics at the University of Wisconsin at Eau Claire. His passion is birds. I just got off the phone talking to Paul. He recently returned from a trip to Belize. Most people from Eau Clare would head to Belize to seek some warmth if spring came late to central Wisconsin. Paul Blanchard had gone to seek out some birds. He photographed over one hundred species of birds on his trip including Trogons, Toucans and hummers.

Paul started camping in The Park in 1977. He often camped in what Mary Ellen Connor called, "the meadow," in the 700 and 800 numbered sites at Nicolet Bay. In the late 1970's, Paul and the Connors would often be the only people camped in this area the first week in June. This was a good place to watch birds.

Since 1977 Paul has been doing a count of Redstart nests along the north shore of Nicolet Bay. The female Redstart maintains a one hundred foot diameter territory. If Paul finds a female, he knows a nest is nearby. In 1977 he counted thirty nests in this area. Last year he found six. The loss of winter nesting habitat in South America and collisions with the ever increasing numbers of cell phone and other communication towers is contributing to the Redstart decline.

Paul would devote every bit of the daylight hours to the pursuit of birds. Paul kept his food in a carrier on top of his van to keep it safe from the raccoons. Paul didn't waste precious time setting up breakfast at the picnic table. He would get a box of cereal from his carrier and eat standing up along side the van. He used pie filling on his cereal in place of milk. If Paul heard an interesting bird call, one that he particularly needed to observe, he could stop in the middle of a conversation, disappear down the road in search of the elusive bird and upon his return, pick up the conversation right where it had left off. Paul is into birds.

The Park is probably the best spot in Door County or anywhere else, to see warblers during the spring migration. It's the warblers that draw Paul Blanchard to The Park. I saw him at Weborg Point a few years ago along with at least 20 other warbler watchers. Paul had a video camera and was intently filming a bird. I relayed some news from Mary Ellen Connor. All the time we conversed, Paul never took his eyes off his bird.

We used to see examples of Paul's photography at Schreiber's store in Fish Creek after Ed Schreiber had sold the business to Mr. Norz. You can still see a good collection of his warbler photos at the nature center.

We hope to see Paul in May when we will be camped at Weborg Point. I'm sure he will be there for this year's warbler migration. Toward the end of our conversation, I told Paul that Mary Ellen Connor had died this past fall. It's not long a human lives. So many birds, so little time. I look forward to seeing Paul's photos from Belize.

Thirty-seven

The Other Superintendents

Ralf Halverson served as The Park superintendent from 1968 to 1974. Ralf had worked for Al Doolittle in the early 1940's, then served three years in the Military in World War II. He returned to The Park in 1946 for a short time and then was sent to Ontario, Wisconsin, to develop Wildcat Mountain State Park. In 1950 he was transferred to Devil's Lake State Park. His wife Dorothy hated to move from her "mountain top" at Ontario down into the valley at Devil's Lake. But Devil's Lake proved to be a good place to raise their family. Ralf was transferred to Peninsula State Park to become the superintendent replacing Lowell Hanson in 1968.

Dorothy recalls that Ralf wanted The Park to retain a natural look. He did not want it to look like a groomed city park. Ralf never left The Park in the summer. The summers were hectic when the park filled with campers, but the other seasons were a little less stressful.

The first year they lived in The Park, a boy who worked at the golf course brought a fawn he had found to Ralf. It was too late to go looking for the mother. Ralf brought the fawn home and Dorothy named her Penny. They kept Penny for the summer in a pen out back of the superintendent's house. In October, when the campers had left The Park, Ralf considered it safe to return Penny to the wild. Penny came back the first few nights to sleep in her pen. Once, Ralf spotted her in the woods. He whistled and she came up to the truck. But after that, she never came up to either of them again. The transition back to the wild had been a success.

Ralf Halverson retired in 1974. He and Dorothy moved to Ephraim. But when the children came to visit, what did they do? They went camping in The Park!

Lynn Hanson was The Park manager for twenty-seven years working for three different superintendents; first Bill Beckstrom, then Lowell Hanson and finally Ralf Halvorsen. Lynn was not only the assistant to the superintendent, but he was also the crew leader for the large staff The Park employed. The Park was mostly self-contained and was equipped to do just about anything.

When Lynn retired, he received an award from Governor Pat Lucy and a letter of appreciation from Harold Jordal, the chairman of the Natural Resources Board. He was honored for the great loyalty he received from the hundreds of workers he had supervised over the years. He was honest, sincere and showed great enthusiasm for his work.

Tom Blackwood is the current park superintendent and claims he is getting close to retirement. But like the Halversons, the Blackwoods are not moving very far. Tom plans to build a retirement home near Fish Creek.

Thirty-eight

The Reservation System

Thursday, April 15, 1999, was the first day the new Wisconsin telephone campsite reservation system went into operation. I called the game, "Dialing for Campsites." I knew it would be difficult to win the game that year. Thousands of campsite reservation requests used to be submitted early in January on the first day you could mail in your reservation form for the year. What would happen when all these people started calling the new reservation system all at once?

I called the number at 7 A.M. I heard a recording saying they would be open for business at 9 A.M. as advertised. I called again at eight and already got a busy signal. I started in earnest one minute before nine. If I was fast with my fingers using the redial feature, I could dial 1-888-WI-PARKS seven times a minute. The race was on!

The first half-hour was not too bad. After that, my left ear started to hurt. I wondered if I could sue the DNR for hearing loss.

10 A.M. I kept pressing the keys. Now both ears hurt. Time dragged. 11 A.M. I had been at this only two hours! I was starting to hallucinate! I was wondering if I could keep it up until 4 P.M. when Carol would get home from school and be able to give me some relief. If we could alternate each hour, I might be able to continue this marathon until the reservation system closed for the day. But then I would have to pick it up again at 9 A.M. the next day. I pressed on.

I envisioned a smoking phone switch somewhere with perplexed technicians wondering what could have caused the meltdown.

I began to wonder about my phone. It was a cordless. What if the battery starts to get low? This was the only touch tone phone in the house with redial! Our other two phones had ancient rotary dials. I shuddered to think about dialing 1-888-WI-PARKS each time using a rotary dialer. I glanced at the clock. It was 11:52 A.M.

I hit redial for the one thousand two hundred and fourth time since 9:00 A.M. RING! RING! I couldn't believe it - I was not getting a busy signal. RING! RING! A person answered! Scott asked if he could help me make a reservation! I had my site list with prioritized numbers laid out in front of me. My Visa card was ready. I gave Scott the information he requested. He said I could get a site for the days I wanted. I told Scott that I had a few particular sites in mind. He asked me for the numbers. I started with 636. He said it was available. I had won the lottery!

My hand was shaking as I replaced the phone in the charging cradle. I gave our dog Ben a big hug. I left a voice mail for Carol at school with the good news. Then I clenched both fists and let out a big, YES! We would be on our honeymoon site for our 29th anniversary.

I remember when getting a campsite wasn't a concern. In 1950, when I first camped in The Park with my parents, there were no specific campsites, only designated campgrounds. You could pitch your tent anywhere in the campground. But each year, the campgrounds got a little more crowded. But nevertheless, everyone packed themselves in. Tents were so close together your ropes often crossed those of your neighbor. Dad used to joke that he didn't have to put in any stakes for his ropes. He would simply tie off to stakes that were already there! Audrey Koch filled out a page for the memory book at the nature center in 1999. Audrey first camped in The Park in 1935 at the age of six. Audrey wrote, "We made friends quickly because our tent ropes would cross those of others and we could hear them snore at night!"

Over the years, the competition for a campsite steadily increased. At first, sites were issued on a first come first served basis. If my father was lucky, he could find one of his desired sites open when we arrived on Saturday. A desired site was any of the sites on the water north of the boat launching ramp in Nicolet Bay. One of Father's favorites was site 644. But the competition for these sites intensified each year. We started leaving home on Friday night, stopping at a motel anywhere between Two Rivers and Algoma. Father would set the alarm clock to get an early start so we could be an hour or two ahead of the Milwaukee crowd and further ahead of the Illinois bunch. One year, after arriving at The Park, dad found a couple young boys camped on 644. A twenty dollar bill convinced them to move.

Often, my father's favorite site was occupied on Saturday, but would become available on Sunday. We would stay at a motel Saturday night. My father would get up at 4 A.M., fill the thermos with coffee and head for The Park office with his folding chair. He would be in line by five waiting for the office to open. Even then he sometimes was not first in line.

As competition continued to increase, even numbered sites could be reserved by mail. At that time, there were three even numbered sites on the water north of the boat launch ramp in Nicolet Bay. Later on, these sites were renumbered so all the shore sites were even numbered and could be reserved. I joined the mail lottery each year, mailing my reservation on the first possible day in January. I got a coveted "north shore" site just once. If you were not lucky enough to get your favorite site in the "mail lottery," you played the "transfer list shuffle" game. Odd numbered sites were still assigned on a first come first served basis. If your favorite odd numbered site was not available, but would be in a day or so, you could set up in another site and put your name on the transfer list. There were four odd numbered sites on my coveted "north shore." Each morning at The Park office, beginning promptly at 10 A.M., those on the transfer list were given first choice of sites opening that day. If your site was not available, you could remain on the transfer list, moving up as others ahead of you got a site they wanted.

The "Transfer List Shuffle" worked for Carol and me for a few years. We honeymooned on site 633 (now site 636) in 1970 and this of course was our favorite site. Using the "transfer list shuffle" we were able to get our favorite site usually within a day or so of arriving at The Park. But others were learning to do "the shuffle." Don and Mary Ellen Connor, from Rockford, Illinois, discovered "the transfer list shuffle" and made an improvement they called "the system." The sites north of the boat launching ramp in Nicolet Bay opened permanently for camping the Thursday after Memorial Day. The Connors would arrive at The Park a few days before these sites opened and set up in what they called, "the meadow," the large open area comprised of the campsites in the 700 and 800 series at Nicolet Bay. Trees now mostly fill that meadow. By the time we got to The Park, the Connors were already number one on the transfer list waiting for site 633 to open. My wife was a teacher. School usually ended a few days after Memorial Day. The Connors, being retired, held the advantage.

Then a miracle occurred. The Connors decided they liked site 631 (now site 634) better than our honeymoon site. We were in luck but only for one year. Dan and Marian Villano, from Cicero, Illinois discovered "the system." The Villanos liked site 633. We beat the Villanos to the transfer list a couple of years so they adopted the Connor's tactics. The Villano's sons, Lenny and Steve, would arrive, as did the Connors, a few days before the sites in north Nicolet Bay opened and would get on the transfer list. By the time Carol and I got to The Park, the Connors were #1 and the Villanos were #2 on the transfer list. The Connors would take site 631 and the Villanos 633.

Once, we arrived at the Park the day before the sites on the north shore in Nicolet Bay opened. We put our name on the transfer list. We were #4. The Connor's were #1, the Villano's were #2. A gent with a motor home was #3. We knew which sites the Connor's and Villano's had in mind. There was only one other odd numbered site, 639, on the water in north Nicolet Bay. I was disappointed because I was sure that #3 on the transfer list would ask for 639 . Carol told me not to worry. She designated the #3 person on the list ahead of us as being "Mr. Full Hook-up." She surmised he was waiting for one of the "full hook-up" sites at Weborg. We stood outside the office at 10 A.M. The Connors chose 631. The Villanos chose 633. Mr. Full Hook-up was next. I was praying - not 639. Please not 639. Mr. Full Hook-up asked for 110. Whew! We were on the shore at Nicolet Bay once again.

The "illegal ladies" were four "ladies" that also liked site 633. I believe they were teachers and like Carol and myself, could not get to The Park early enough in June to be assured of getting site 633. One of the ladies had a daughter living in the area. One year, the daughter pitched a tent on an open site about a week before Memorial Day and before site 633 had opened for the season. She put her name on the transfer list. By the time we got to The Park the daughter was ahead of us on the list. When site 633 opened after Memorial Day, she took it and the four "illegal ladies" moved in. The daughter never occupied the site she took while remaining on the transfer list and never stayed at 633 once the ladies moved in. We could have complained. It was and still is illegal to obtain a site for another person. But then, I wouldn't have this story to tell.

Managing the transfer list and putting up with the antics of people like Carol and me, the Connors and the Villanos that "worked this system" to get a coveted shore site is probably what led to the Park to renumber all the sites on the water in Nicolet Bay to be even numbered sites and thus capable of being reserved using the mail reservation system at the time. So now you know why all the shore sites in Nicolet Bay have even numbers.

As my parents got older, they gave up camping, but would often stay at a motel in the area for a few days while Carol and I were camping in The Park. Most of the time, I had a shore site on Nicolet Bay. But I remember my father coming into camp one year when we had to take a site "on the wrong side of the road."   As Father strode into camp, he remarked, "I see you had to settle with the poor folks this year." I remarked, "at least we were IN The Park."

Today, you can make a reservation up to eleven months in advance on the internet as well as by telephone. This is a good system. No, you may not get your favorite site at your favorite time, but if you reserve early, at least you will "be in The Park!" Weekends go fast! But you can often get in during the week.

After I had my site booked that memorable day in 1999 when the telephone reservation system went into operation, I called the Connors. Don was trying to get through dialing a few times each hour. He finally got through on the third day and got their beloved site 631. Seventy percent of the reservation center calls that year were requests for sites at Peninsula State Park.

There really IS something more difficult to reserve than a campsite in The Park. Try getting a burial plot in Blossomburg Cemetery! Carol and I often thought our final campsite should be in this beautiful cemetery. The last plot at Blossomburg was sold about 15 years ago. But I guessed that from time to time, previously purchased plots may come up for sale. We inquired at the Gibraltar Town office in Fish Creek this past year.   The town clerk has a waiting list of over 100 people. To even get on this list, you must be a property owner in the Township. I wonder if I can arrange to have my ashes scattered from the top of Eagle Tower.

Thirty-nine

The Later Years

My years of camping with my parents ended in 1969 when I went into the Navy. For another decade, my mother and father still camped in The Park each summer. They often took my two nephews along. After my father gave up camping, he and my mother would visit Carol and me for a few days each time we vacationed in The Park. Sometimes, they would pick up Carol's parents in Chicago and bring them along. They would stay at a motel. But the motel was only for sleeping. My father arrived at our camp early each morning for a camp breakfast. While I cooked bacon and eggs, he would get a fire going to do some toast. There is nothing like toast made over an open campfire. When my dad visited us in camp, I tried on numerous occasions to cook chicken like he used to do over the campfire. My father always said it was good, but we both knew it was not equal to that done by the real master of cooking chicken over cedar coals. I could only make amends by suggesting we head to Wilson's after dinner for a soda.

I never saw my father cry, but on two occasions, I did see him having trouble choking back the tears. The first time was when he dropped me off at the military induction center in Chicago in 1969. The last time, was when he left our camp after having had a camp breakfast. He had already checked out of the motel and was going to head for home. It was a beautiful day, perfectly clear, a little chop on the water, the birches stood out against the dark blue sky. Carol's parents were along on that trip. My father was blinking furiously to hide the tears. My mother-in-law told me later that it was very quiet trip all the way back to Chicago. Our parents are gone now. What I wouldn't give for another camp breakfast with our folks.

Carol and I still camp in The Park. We like early May and late October when everything in Door County is a little less crowded. We camped in a tent until 2002 when we bought a small trailer. I intend to continue to camp as long as I can in this enchanted place I still simply call, The Park.

Forty

The Future

Sigurd Olson (1899-1982) was a wilderness writer and preservationist. In 1925, he helped lead a successful battle to have one million acres in northern Minnesota set aside to be preserved as the Boundary Waters Canoe Area Wilderness. The struggle to preserve this wilderness continues today, as does the struggle to preserve all the places where we can still experience nature. The 3,800 acres we call Peninsula State Park is one of these places.

Thousands of visitors each year experience what John Nolan believed was the purpose of a park. The park staff can work to eradicate exotics like garlic mustard from The Park. They can work to protect the park from the emerald ash borer. But they have little influence over the earth's environment which is the greatest long term threat to The Park.

In a video titled, "The Wilderness World of Sigurd F. Olson," Sigurd responds to a question young people ask concerning the future. Sigurd is standing at a beautiful spot among huge trees. One of Sigurd's hands is on an enormous tree hundreds of years old; the other grasps a small sapling. Sigurd says the enormous tree represents his generation, while the young sapling represents the younger generation. Sigurd looks at the huge old tree he is standing next to and then at the small sapling at his feet. He proclaims that at one time, the world depended on these huge trees. But now it depends on the little sapling. The young people, just like the little sapling, have an important task to perform.

The new generation must carry on the battle to preserve beautiful places such as the one where Sigurd is standing. It's not just a battle to preserve places anymore, but a battle to preserve the earth from man-made environmental threats. The battle goes on endlessly.

John Nolan wanted Peninsula State Park to be a place where nature could be preserved and people could come to refresh, strengthen and renew their spirit. Many superintendents, along with their staff, have presided over this park allowing generations of people to be refreshed by its beauty. Now the younger generation must take up the task of preserving The Park so it will always be a place where people can come to renew their spirit.

A moment of calm, Carol and Ben, on the shore of Nicolet Bay, renewing their spirits.

Forty-one

The Sources

The Photographs

All photographs are the author's except where noted.

1-The Introduction

The line from the Song, "Old Winds" Copyright 1996 by the Nelson-Ferris Concert Company used with permission by Warren Nelson. Old Winds is one song from the program, "Riding The Wind," an illustrated Musical History of Bayfield and the Apostle Islands. "Riding the Wind" is performed each summer by The Lake Superior Big Top Chautauqua, Washburn, Wisconsin.

2-The Geology

Palmquist, John C. editor. Wisconsin's Door Peninsula A Natural History. Copyright 1989. Perin Press, 226 E. College Avenue, Appleton, Wisconsin 54911. 196 pages.
ISBN# 0-929682-00-9

3-The Native Americans

Palmquist, John C. editor. Wisconsin's Door Peninsula A Natural History. Copyright 1989. Perin Press, 226 E. College Avenue, Appleton, Wisconsin 54911. 196 pages.
ISBN# 0-929682-00-9

Charles, Craig. Exploring Door County. NorthWord Press, Box 1360, Minocqua, WI 54548. 212 pages. ISBN 1-55971-011

Dirst, Victoria. An Archaeological Survey at the Shanty Bay Site in Peninsula State Park, Door County, Wisconsin. Wisconsin Department of Natural Resources Bureau of Property Management. November 13, 1990.

3-The Native Americans (continued)

Harden, Carol. The Indian Memorial Pole. Published by The Door County Historical Society. 1971.

1994 Drums Along the Rock Native American Pow Wow program.

4-The History B.P. (Before Park)

Holand, Hjalmar, R. History of Door County, Wisconsin. Copyright 1917 by Hjalmar R. Holand. Reprinted by Wm Claxton Ltd, Ellison Bay, Wisconsin. 1993. Volume I, 459 pages. ISBN 0-940473-23-2

Lotz, Marvin M. Discovering Door County's Past. Copyright 1994. Holly House Press, Fish Creek, Wisconsin. 458 pages.

Nolen, John, "State Parks for Wisconsin" 1909. (PAR.2:N 54) Online facsimile at: http://www.wisconsinhistory.org/turningpoints/search.asp?id=1188

5-The Land

Dirst, Victoria. An Archaeological Survey for a new septic system in Peninsula State Park, Door County Wisconsin. Wisconsin Department of Natural Resources Bureau of Property Management. October 17, 1990

Holand, Hjalmar, R. History of Door County, Wisconsin. Copyright 1917 by Hjalmar R. Holand. Reprinted by Wm Claxton Ltd, Ellison Bay, Wisconsin, 1993. Volume I, 459 pages. ISBN 0-940473-23-2

Sholem, Stanford H. Horseshoe Island, The Folda Years. Copyright 1998. The Ephraim Foundation, Inc. Ephraim, Wisconsin. 128 pages. ISBN: 0-9659006-1-4

6-Al Doolittle

Ed Schreiber. Interview by the author, June 9, 1992 (Besides that material directly cited, this interview was the source for much of the information concerning people who lived in various cabins and residences in The Park.)

Dorothy Halvorsen. Interview by the author, February 26, 2006

"Early Days in Peninsula State Park' by Jay Doolittle. Contained in Fish Creek Echoes. Edited by Virginia Kinsey and Edward Schreiber. Copyright 2000. Published by John and Nancy Sargent, Fish Creek, Wisconsin. 353 pages. ISBN: 0-615-11236-6 (information about superintendent's house and use of fire towers)

1999 Peninsula State Park Visitor article, "Park offers towering view for over 80 years." (information concerning towers at The Park)

State of Wisconsin Conservation Commission – Bulletin 3 – Working Plan for Forest Lands of Peninsula State Park Door County Wisconsin. Madison, Wisconsin 1917. State Of Wisconsin Historical Library, Madison, Wisconsin.

Gerhard Miller. Interview by the author, June 11, 1991.

Door County Advocate, March 21, 1961. "Cottage Built Around Cooper's Fireplace Gone." (information concerning Gatter cottage)

Fish Creek – The Summertime. Compiled by Libby Isham and Betsy Guenzel. Volume I, 1991. Copy Available at the Fish Creek Library

7-Horseshoe Island

Ellis, William S. "A Kingdom So Delicious." National Geographic Magazine, March 1969. (Information about the Utopia)

Sholem, Stanford H. Horseshoe Island, The Folda Years. Copyright 1998 by The Ephraim Foundation, Inc. Ephraim, Wisconsin. 128 pages. ISBN 0-9659006-1-4

8-The Lighthouse

Badtke, Francis. <u>Eagle Lighthouse</u>. Copyright 1964 by Francis Badtke. Printed by Door County Publishing Company, Sturgeon Bay Wisconsin.

Website: <u>www.midwestconnection.com</u>

Website:
<u>www.terrypepper.com/lights/michigan/eaglebluf/eaglbluff.htm</u>

9-The Golf Course

Reminiscences of Twenty Years Activity of a Community Club. Ephraim Men's Club. April 8, 1932. A copy exists in the history book at the Park Nature Center.

Burton, Paul and Frances. <u>Ephraim Stories</u>. Copyright 1999 by Paul and Francis Burton. Stonehill Publishing, P.O. Box 250, Ephraim, Wisconsin. 316 pages. ISBN: 0-9650769-1-1
(historic information about the original golf course, club house and screened in porch)

10-Camp Meenahga

Door County Almanak # 5 Copyright 1990. The Dragonsbreath Press, Sister Bay, Wisconsin. 350 pages.

Alice Clark Peddle in "Fish Creek – The Summertime" – stories collected by Libby Isham and Betsy Guenzel. Volume I 1991. Located at Fish Creek Library.

Pieces of the Past – Duncan Thorp – Recorded by his Daughter, Pamela Thorp Sarett. 1987. Copy at Fish Creek Library.

Park Historic Sign located at the site of Camp Meenahga.

11-The Fire

The Thorps 1832-1932 by Duncan Thorp. Copy at Fish Creek Library

Fish Creek – The Summertime. Compiled by Libby Isham and Betsy Guenzel. Volume I, 1991. Copy Available at the Fish Creek Library

12-The Memorial Pole

Burton, Paul and Frances. <u>Ephraim Stories</u>. Copyright 1999 by Paul and Francis Burton. Stonehill Publishing, P.O. Box 250, Ephraim, Wisconsin. 316 pages. ISBN: 0-9650769-1-1

The Peninsula, Volume 9, Summer 1991. "Indian Monument" by Jane Shea, "Indian Memorial" by Jane Shea, and "Dedication of Indian Memorial Pole" transcript of a speech given by Harold Holand at the dedication of the Indian Memorial Pole on September 12, 1970. Copyright 1971 by the Door County Historical Society, Sturgeon Bay, Wisconsin.

Door County Advocate, July 15, 1969. "Indian memorial location Tempest on a totem pole."

Door County Advocate, July 31, 1969. "State Agrees – Memorial pole will be on original site."

Tschekatch'ake'mau III. Recollections of Chief Roy J. Oshkosh by John H. Taube and Thomas Kanzenbach.

Gerhard Miller. Interview by the author, June 11, 1991. (Information concerning Charles Lesaar)

13-The CCC Camp

Ahlgren, Carol Ann. "A human and landscape architectural legacy: the influence of the Civilian Conservation Corps on Wisconsin state park development." M.A. Thesis, University of Wisconsin. Madison, Wisconsin. 1987. 145 pages.

13-The CCC Camp (continued)

Door County Advocate, November 24, 1933. "Jobs for 125 Men in 2 State Parks"

Door County Advocate, March 2, 1934. "Peninsula Park is Building Big Dock"

Door County Advocate, February 13, 1935. "C.C.C. Camp for County is Sought"

Door County Advocate, May 10, 1935. "County Allocated New C.C.C. Camp"

Door County Advocate, March 20, 1936. Club Criticizes CCC Work in Park"

Door County Advocate, May 15, 1936. "Investigates CCC in Peninsula Park"

The National Association of Civilian Conservation Corps Alumni (NACCCA) web site: www.cccalumni.org

14-The Game Farm

Wisconsin Conservation Commission, State Park Pamphlets, Madison Wisconsin. 1931

15-The Prohibition

Burton, Paul and Frances. Ephraim Stories. Copyright 1999 by Paul and Francis Burton. Stonehill Publishing, P.O. Box 250, Ephraim, Wisconsin. 316 pages. ISBN: 0-9650769-1-1 (Information concerning taverns in The Park)

16-The Huber Theater

Door County Advocate, August 17, 1934. "1,500 at Camp Show in Park: Stage Dedicated to Producer"

17-The Ski Jump

Door County Advocate, June 7, 1935. "Ski Slide Expert Visits Park"

Door County Advocate, July 12, 1935. "Winter Sports to be Pushed by Club"

Door County Advocate, September 20, 1935, "Amateur Winter Sports Planned"

Door County Advocate, November 29, 1935. "Winter Sports Club Seeking to Get Slides Made in State Park"

Door County Advocate, February 21, 1936. "Ski and Toboggan Slide Plans Done"

Door County Advocate, December 18, 1936. "Ski Jumpers Say Slide Dangerous"

19-The POW Camp

Thomas C. Blackwood e-mail of July 26, 2001 relating information per Dorothy Halverson concerning the location of the POW camp. Copy in History book at the Nature Center.

Door County Advocate, March 30, 1945. "2,000 German PW's May Come Here for the Fruit Harvest"

Door County Advocate, April 20, 1945. "German Prisoners of War Still Awaited"

Door County Advocate, April 20, 1945. "Federation of Labor Protesting PW's"

Door County Advocate, May 18, 1945. "German War Prisoner Camp Set Up Here"

Door County Advocate, May 25, 1945. "Curiosity Running High Over German PW's Here"

19-The POW Camp (continued)

Door County Advocate, July 13, 1945. "2,000 PW's Coming To Harvest Cherries"

Door County Advocate, August 17, 1945. "Cherries Off Trees, Picker Camps Close"

Door County Advocate, August 31, 1945. "PW's Earned Over $100,000 for U.S."

27-Putting The Ladies Down

Helen Richter. Interview by the author, May 16, 1992.

31-The Three Week Rule

Ed Schreiber. Interview by the author, June 9, 1992

Marge and Ernie Krubsack. Interview by the author, November 3, 1991

Clerk of Courts Records, Door County Courthouse, Sturgeon Bay, Wisconsin (Information on subdivisions of Carl Anderson Property)

Door County Advocate, October 7, 1976. Carl Anderson Obituary

31-Trouble In The Park

Door County Advocate, July 7, 1967. "Holiday youth problem drawing heavy fire here"

Lynn Hanson. Interview by the author, June 12, 1992

36-The Other Docks

Malcolm D. Vail, <u>Tales of Ephraim Waters</u>. Ephraim Yacht Club. Copyright 1956 by the Ephraim Foundation, Inc. Ephraim, WI 28 pages (Information concerning the Hanson dock)

38-The Other Superintendents

Lynn Hanson. Interview by the author, June 12, 1992

Dorothy Halverson. Interview by the author, February 26, 2006

41-The Future

The Wilderness World of Sigurd F. Olson. NorthWord Inc. Ashland WI 54806. ISBN 0-942802-16-0 VHS 28 minutes

Entropy

When the present day Eagle Tower was raised in the 1930s, a tree in the woods off toward the Eagle Terrace side served as an anchor for the rig used to hoist the center pole. The stump of this tree with a piece of the cable remains

Entropy - the process, where things that have been built by man or by nature, eventually degrade back to their original state.